MYRON WINGEN

DISCIPLINING KIDS TO BE GOD-FEARING

A Workbook for Raising Children Who Connect with God

DISCLAIMER

The information provided in this workbook is intended for educational and informational purposes only, to assist parents in their journey of raising children. It is not intended as a substitute for professional advice from a licensed therapist, counselor, pediatrician, or other qualified child development specialist.

While the exercises and guidance in this workbook can be helpful for improving communication with your children, resolving family conflict, and strengthening parent-child relationships, they are not intended to diagnose or treat any specific behavioral or developmental challenges in children.

If you are experiencing significant challenges in your parenting journey or have concerns about your child's behavior or development, please seek professional help from a qualified specialist.

The author and publisher are not responsible for any adverse effects or consequences resulting from the use of this workbook.

Thank you for choosing this workbook! I'm excited that you're taking this step towards raising children who are grounded in their faith and connected to God's love.

Your willingness to invest in your parenting journey and prioritize your children's spiritual development is inspiring. I believe that by actively engaging with the exercises and reflections in this workbook, you can strengthen your family bonds, navigate parenting challenges with grace, and create a home where faith flourishes.

Remember, parenting is a lifelong adventure that requires constant learning, growing, and relying on God's guidance. This workbook is your companion on this journey, providing you with biblical principles and practical tools to cultivate a God-centered home where your children can thrive.

I appreciate your trust in me and wish you all the best on your journey towards raising children who love and honor God.

With warm regards,

Myron Wingen.

This workbook belongs to

____

____

Dedication

To my fellow parents:

They strive daily to inculcate in their children a love and understanding of God. I hope this book encourages and guides you as you navigate the joys and challenges of parenting.

May it inspire you to raise a family in which faith thrives and children interact with God in profound and meaningful ways.

Acknowledgement

This workbook would not exist without the support and encouragement of many people.

First, I'd like to thank my friends and fellow parents who shared their stories and insights. Your openness about the struggles and triumphs of raising children brought these pages to life.

I'm also grateful for the community that supported me, the late-night conversations that generated ideas, and the early-morning writing sessions fueled by strong coffee and the need to put those ideas into words.

Finally, I thank God for providing the motivation and strength to achieve this task. May this workbook serve His purpose and bring glory to His Name.

Why This Workbook?

Perhaps you choose this workbook based on a specific difficulty level. Maybe disobedience runs across your family, or sibling squabbles occur daily. Possibly you just want to deepen your faith-based relationship with your kids.

Whatever brought you here, this workbook offers a path forward. It's not a magical solution, but a guide to help you:

- Understand: Develop a solid understanding of biblical discipline, transitioning from punishment to a heart-centered approach.
- Connect: Build stronger, more trusting relationships with your children.
- Act: Discover practical ways to overcome everyday problems with confidence and grace.
- Grow: Make faith a living, breathing part of your family's daily routine, not just on Sundays.

This workbook provides a basis for action. Inside, you will find:

- Real-world examples: Discover how other parents handled similar challenges and found solutions.
- Reflection Questions: Examine your attitudes and behaviors toward discipline.
- Practical exercises allow you to practice new skills through step-by-step activities.
- Scriptural insights: Base your parenting on your understanding of God's Word.

This workbook is for you if you're ready to go from irritability to calmness, from reaction to intention. Let us begin.

Contents

Introduction

My son, Ethan, recently decided it would be a good idea to redecorate our living room wall using a permanent marker. Ethan is now a bright, vivacious five-year-old with a wicked streak that spans a mile. He's also at the age where the world is his painting and any space calls for a splash of color. Unfortunately, his artistic approach did not align with my house design choices.

As I glanced at the massive black picture on my freshly painted wall, a wave of wrath came over me. My initial reaction was to raise my voice, scold him for his disobedience, and administer an immediate punishment. After all, hadn't I frequently told him not to draw on the wall? But, when I looked at Ethan, his small frame shaking slightly and his eyes wide with horror and defiance, I paused. Something about his expression caused me to stop in my tracks.

At that time, I realized that reacting in anger would just intensify the situation and create more distance between us. It would not teach him about duty or respect. Instead, it would further heighten his dread of making mistakes and desire to keep things from me.

I took a deep breath, knelt to his level, and quietly inquired about what had happened. He apologized, just above a whisper, and said that he was attempting to draw a portrait of my family. He wanted to surprise me with some beautiful artwork, but he couldn't find any paper.

As I listened to his explanation, my rage faded and was replaced by a surge of sympathy. I saw a tiny boy with a big heart who had made a mistake, not a defiant child intent on breaking the rules. He had not intended to demolish our house; he had simply behaved rashly, driven by his creative spirit and a desire to please me.

Instead of criticizing him, I recognized his good intentions and thanked him for wanting to create something unique for me. Then we discussed how vital it is to respect our belongings and sketch with appropriate tools. We discussed the difference between making mistakes and willfully disobeying, and I informed him that it is okay to make mistakes as long as we learn from them.

We found a pail of soapy water and sponges and started cleaning the wall. It took some work, but the marker stains eventually faded, leaving only a faint trace of Ethan's artistic adventure. More importantly, it strengthened our friendship, increased our understanding of one another, and taught us an essential lesson.

This experience reminded me that discipline is more than just correcting behavior; it is also about teaching our children to be more conscious of themselves, their environment, and their relationship with God. It is about teaching children to make sound decisions, accept responsibility for their actions, and build character and integrity.

As Christian parents, it is our honor and responsibility to raise our children in the Lord's way. This includes not only educating them about God's love and instructions but also demonstrating those values in our own lives, notably via how we discipline our children.

God's Word provides us with a foundation for discipline based on love, grace, and wisdom. It teaches us to correct our children with kindness and understanding, to guide them gently but firmly, and to constantly point them to Christ's hope and forgiveness.

When we handle discipline in this way, we create an environment in which our children are comfortable making mistakes, learning from them, and growing in their faith. We show that God's love is unconditional, even when they falter, and that His grace is always available to help them get back on track.

This approach to discipline is not always straightforward. It invites us to put aside our frustrations and look at our children with compassion, responding with patience and understanding. However, the benefits are great.

When we discipline our children in a way that reflects God's love, we shape their behavior while also nurturing their hearts. We build a foundation of trust and respect that will serve them well throughout their lives. Most importantly, we help them form a deep and abiding connection with God, a connection that will carry them through life's challenges and lead them to a future full of purpose and meaning.

This workbook is designed to help you, as a Christian parent, put these ideas into practice. It will provide you with practical tools and tactics for dealing with discipline in a way that reflects God's love and wisdom. It will challenge you to examine your own heart and motivations, as well as encourage you to create a household where religion thrives and children flourish.

As you read these pages, understand that you are not alone. God is with you every step of the way, guiding, strengthening, and empowering you to raise your children in a way that honors Him.

May this be a time of growth and discovery for you and your children as you learn to follow the Lord's ways.

How to Use This Workbook

This workbook is designed to be a practical resource for Christian parents who want their children to connect with God. It includes exercises, reflections, and action steps to help you implement the principles taught.

Here are some ways to make the most of it:

- Go at your own pace. Work through the chapters in order, or move ahead to the sections that address your most pressing issues.

- Reflect honestly. Take some time to consider the questions and exercises. Be open to new ideas and viewpoints.

- Put it into practice. Don't just read the text; take action! Implement the ideas and suggestions in your daily parenting.

- Make it yours. Feel free to scribble in the margins, underline important sections, and customize the exercises to your family's individual needs.

- Share with others. Consider working through this workbook with a spouse, friend, or small group. Discussion and shared experiences might help the learning process.

Above all, approach this experience with an open heart and a desire to grow. May God bless you as you seek to teach His love and knowledge to your children.

Chapter 1: Understanding Biblical Discipline

"Discipline your children, for in that there is hope; do not be a willing party to their death." Proverbs 19:18 (NIV)

This verse, despite its harsh language, gets to the heart of why we, as Christian parents, punish. It is not about punishment or control, but about survival. It is about leading our children away from destructive roads and into a life filled with hope, purpose, and a close relationship with God.

However, what exactly defines biblical discipline? How does it differ from the prevalent understanding of discipline? How can we, as flawed parents, implement these ideas in our own homes?

In a culture that typically connects discipline with punishment, it is easy to lose sight of its true meaning and purpose. We may associate it with harsh words, tight rules, or even physical punishment. However, the biblical idea of discipline paints an entirely different picture.

The term "discipline" is derived from the Greek word "paideia," which has several meanings, including training, instruction, education, and correction. It reflects the idea of nurturing and guiding someone into maturity and wholeness.

Consider a gardener tending to a sprouting tree. They remove dead branches, strengthen the trunk, and ensure the roots receive adequate water and nutrients. They do this not to harm the tree, but rather to help it grow and yield good fruit.

Similarly, biblical discipline is to nourish our children's hearts and minds, guiding them toward a life that values and reflects God's character. It is about preparing them for righteousness, teaching them the truth, and disciplining them with love and patience.

At its core, biblical discipline is based on love. It arises from a desire to see our children grow, to help them reach their full potential, and to guide them to a deep and lasting relationship with God.

This love-centered approach sets biblical discipline apart from worldly systems, which usually concentrate on control, punishment, or even humiliation. While these strategies may result in external cooperation, they typically fail to address the underlying issue. They may instill hostility, resistance, or feelings of worthlessness in our children.

In contrast, biblical discipline seeks to address the root cause of a problem rather than just its symptoms. It recognizes that disobedience is often a cry for help, implying that something deeper is going on in a child's heart.

Rather than simply reacting to exterior activities, we are encouraged to delve deeper and understand the underlying needs and motivations that drive our children's behavior. This requires cultivating empathy, paying close attention, and asking probing questions to better understand their point of view.

When we approach discipline from a place of love and understanding, we create a climate in which our children feel comfortable opening up, discussing their struggles, and seeking our assistance. We build trust and respect, allowing us to bring the truth into their lives, even if it is difficult.

Another distinguishing element of biblical discipline is the emphasis on grace. We are called to show grace to our children in the same way that God forgives us and gives us a fresh start.

This does not imply that we ignore or condone their misbehavior. It suggests that we accept that they are fallible, just like us, and will make mistakes. It entails offering them forgiveness, second chances, and the opportunity to learn and develop from their mistakes.

When our children believe they are unconditionally loved, even when they make errors, they are more open to receiving criticism. They are less likely to feel defensive or discouraged, and they are more likely to follow the counsel we offer.

Grace also influences our approach to punishment. We must acknowledge that we, as parents, are not flawless. We will make mistakes, lose patience, and say things we later regret.

In those situations, it is vital to model humility and repentance for our children. We must be willing to own our flaws, seek forgiveness, and demonstrate that we are all on a journey of growth and learning.

This sincerity not only strengthens our bond with our children but also teaches them the importance of taking responsibility for their actions and seeking forgiveness when they have caused harm to others.

Finally, biblical discipline emphasizes training and instruction. It's more than just addressing poor behavior; it's about actively teaching our children God's Word, instilling a desire for truth in them, and equipping them to make sound decisions.

This takes more than just going to church on Sundays or praying before bedtime. It means bringing faith into all aspects of our family life, resulting in a home where God's presence is felt, His Word is respected, and His values are upheld.

It requires having regular faith talks, sharing our testimonies, and living a life consistent with our ideals. It means giving our children the opportunity to assist others, see God's love in action, and strengthen their relationship with Him.

This proactive approach to discipline fosters in our children a strong moral compass, a complete understanding of right and wrong, and a desire to serve God in all that they do. It empowers youngsters to face life's challenges with confidence, knowing they have a firm foundation of truth and a loving God to guide them.

Understanding biblical discipline includes not only studying but also changing our hearts and parenting techniques. It is about taking a God-centered perspective and viewing discipline as an opportunity for growth, connection, and spiritual development.

The Loving Purpose of Discipline

The book of Proverbs has a plethora of information on God's design for discipline. Take a look at this scripture: *"My son, do not despise the Lord's discipline, and do not resent his rebuke, because the Lord disciplines those he loves, as a father the son he delights in." (Proverbs 3:11–12 NIV)*

This verse expresses a fundamental truth: God disciplines those He loves. His punishment is not an act of fury or vengeance, but rather a manifestation of His deep love and care for our welfare. God, like a loving father, guides and corrects His children because He desires the best for them.

This concept applies not only to our connection with God but also to our role as parents. When we discipline our children, we are reflecting God's heart, demonstrating His love, and cooperating with Him in their spiritual development.

Another significant chapter in Proverbs is, *"Whoever spares the rod hates their children, but the one who loves their children is careful to discipline them." (Proverbs 13:24; NIV).*

The "rod" in this context refers to any sort of discipline, not only physical punishment. The emphasis here is on the importance of consistent and compassionate discipline. A parent who truly loves their child would not avoid discipline, no matter how painful it is, since they understand that it is vital for their child's growth and well-being.

This lyric challenges the notion that discipline is harsh or harmful. Instead, it promotes punishment as a type of love, a way to protect our children from harm and lead them to a life of virtue.

The author of Hebrews expresses this idea when he writes, *"Endure suffering as discipline; God is treating you as his children." What youngsters are not punished by their father?"If you are not disciplined—and everyone is disciplined—you are not authentic, nor are you true sons and daughters. Hebrews 12:7–8 NIV*

This verse reminds us that discipline is an important part of the Christian life. Discipline helps us mature, develop character, and learn to obey God.

Athletes go through arduous training to achieve their goals, and we must endure the sufferings of discipline to become more like Christ. This could include enduring adversity, making sacrifices, and receiving feedback when we depart from the path.

However, the writer of Hebrews reminds us that God's discipline is not random or harsh. He treats us as His loving children, guiding us with wisdom and care. His discipline is designed to purify, develop, and prepare us for a life of purpose and fulfillment.

These Proverbs and Hebrews chapters highlight a few key components of God's purpose for discipline.

- Discipline is a sign of love. It arises from our drive for personal well-being and growth.

- Discipline is essential for growth. It allows us to grow in character and walk in obedience to God.

- Discipline should be consistent and timely. Misbehavior must be addressed immediately and consistently, taking into account the child's age and knowledge.

- Discipline should be followed by instructions. Corrections should be supported by clear explanations, instructions, and assistance.

- Discipline should be delivered with patience and gentleness. We must approach our children with empathy, understanding, and a willingness to forgive.

- Discipline should finally result in God's love and forgiveness. Our goal is to teach our children that God loves them unconditionally, even when they make mistakes.

These principles provide a framework for understanding and carrying out discipline in a way that honors and reflects God's character. They encourage us to go beyond a purely behavioral approach to punishment, recognizing that our children's hearts must be engaged just as much as their behaviors.

God's aim for discipline is not to break our children's spirits or force them to obey. It is about nurturing their hearts, guiding their steps, and assisting them in becoming the people God created them to be.

It is about collaborating with God on their spiritual growth, teaching them to love Him, trust Him, and walk in His ways.

As we seek to discipline our children in a God-honoring manner, remember that we are reflecting His heart, demonstrating His love, and participating in His redeeming work.

May us approach this responsibility with humility, wisdom, and a deep faith in His grace.

Biblical Discipline vs. Worldly Methods

In a world that usually values rapid results and outward compliance, the concept of discipline is easily misunderstood. We may find ourselves favoring tactics that emphasize control, discipline, or even manipulation to achieve desirable behaviors in our children. However, a biblical approach to discipline contradicts these worldly tendencies, offering a completely different perspective on how we guide and love our children.

One of the most visible improvements is in the motivation for discipline. Worldly ways can be driven by a desire to regulate a child's behavior for the sake of convenience, social approval, or maintaining order. The emphasis is on outward cooperation while minimizing disruptions to our habits and reputation.

Biblical discipline, on the other hand, derives from a deeper motivation: a desire for the child's ultimate good. It recognizes that true progress and thriving come from an internal transformation of the heart rather than simply adhering to outward rules. It strives to build character, impart insight, and promote a deep, long-term relationship with God.

This difference in motive naturally leads to a divergence in methods. Worldly systems may use external controls to induce conformity, such as rewards, penalties, or even emotional manipulation. While these tactics may have temporary results, they typically fail to address the root causes of misbehavior and may even affect a child's long-term development.

Consider a child who receives constant praise and rewards for good grades. While this appears to be a healthy strategy, it may unintentionally promote reliance on external validation and a fear of failure. The child may become more focused on pleasing others rather than developing a genuine drive to study.

In contrast, biblical discipline emphasizes instruction, correction, and guidance. It seeks to engage a child's heart and mind by guiding them through the reasons for expectations and the consequences of their actions. This method requires clear communication, comprehensive explanations, and consistent follow-through. It requires parents to invest time and effort in building a trustworthy and respectful relationship in which free talk and honest interactions can thrive.

Rather than relying just on rewards or punishments, parents who utilize biblical discipline explain why specific behaviors are essential, how they affect others, and how they align with God's principles. This technique fosters comprehension, increases internal motivation, and enables children to make sound decisions based on their views.

The desired goals of discipline differ significantly between biblical and worldly perspectives. Worldly approaches usually emphasize outward conformity and adherence to social norms. The goal is to raise well-behaved children who fit in, follow the rules, and do not cause trouble.

While these outcomes may be beneficial, they fall short of the transformative goals of biblical discipline. The ultimate goal is not only to modify behavior, but also to develop character, encourage faith, and guide children toward a God-honoring lifestyle.

This includes aiding young people in establishing a strong moral compass, a complete understanding of right and wrong, and a desire to serve God in whatever they do. It comprises teaching youngsters how to make good judgments, accept responsibility for their acts, and seek forgiveness when they fail.

These results aren't always evident or easy to quantify. They may take years to fully manifest as children mature and deepen their faith. However, they are the product of a discipline based on love, grace, and truth, which seeks to shape not only outer actions but also the inner person.

Another key issue is the concept of punishment. While punishment can be an effective form of discipline, it should never be the primary focus. In the modern world, punishment is generally regarded as the principal tool for changing behavior and inflicting pain or anguish to deter future misdeeds.

In contrast, biblical discipline views punishment as a last resort, a tool to be used sparingly and cautiously. The emphasis is on educating, correcting, and guiding, rather than causing pain or guilt.

When punishment is necessary, it should be administered with love and firmness, openly tied to the violation, and proportionate to the offense. It should also explain why the activity was incorrect and how to make better choices in the future.

Punishment is not intended to humiliate or break a child's spirit, but rather to help them understand the natural consequences of their actions and motivate them to change. It is about teaching children to accept responsibility for their acts and make amends when they have harmed others.

Furthermore, biblical discipline highlights the importance of grace and forgiveness. We are called to show grace to our children in the same way that God forgives us and gives us a fresh start. This does not suggest disregarding or supporting their misconduct; rather, it acknowledges that they, like us, are flawed and will make mistakes. It requires giving them forgiveness, second opportunities, and the opportunity to learn from their mistakes.

This strategy creates a loving and welcoming environment in which children feel free to disclose their mistakes and seek help without fear of being condemned. It helps children understand the transformative power of forgiveness, both receiving it from their parents and giving it to others.

Key Points

→ Discipline is built on love, not fury. It is about guiding children's growth and maturity, not punishing them for their faults.

→ Biblical discipline focuses on the heart rather than the actions. It seeks to address the fundamental attitudes and motivations that drive behavior.

→ Grace and forgiveness are essential components of discipline. Children need to know that they are unconditionally loved, even if they make errors.

→ Discipline encompasses both instruction and guidance. It is about teaching young people God's word and equipping them to make sound decisions.

→ Discipline should be administered with gentleness and understanding. It is vital to consider the child's age, developmental stage, and unique needs.

Self-Reflection Questions

1. What is your primary motivation for disciplining your child? Is it to control their behavior or to bring them to God?

2. How does your disciplinary method reflect God's love and grace? Do you provide forgiveness and second chances as freely as God does?

3. How do you balance instruction and correction in your discipline? Do you take the time to explain why you have particular expectations and the consequences of your actions?

4. How do you handle losing patience or making mistakes in your discipline? Do you demonstrate humility and regret to your child?

5. How can you create a more loving and caring environment in which your child can develop and learn? What specific steps can you take to improve your approach to discipline?

Chapter 2: Building a Strong Foundation

"Start children off on the way they should go, and even when they are old they will not turn from it."
Proverbs 22:6 (NIV)

This verse underlines the need to establish a stable foundation in our children's lives. It emphasizes the long-term benefits of early education and the necessity of instilling values that will influence their decisions as they grow into adults. What exactly does it mean to "set children on the right path"? It's more than just establishing rules and enforcing obedience; it's about building a strong and lasting bond that will serve as a firm basis for their spiritual and emotional development.

At the heart of this foundation is the parent-child relationship. It is an ideal environment for trust, respect, and open communication. When this link is strong, children feel comfortable exploring, learning, and growing because they know they have a loving and supportive anchor to lean on.

Trust is a vital component of a healthy parent-child relationship. Children must understand that their parents are reliable, consistent, and trustworthy. They must be certain that their parents will love them unconditionally, even if they make mistakes, and that they can always turn to their parents for support and counsel.

Building trust requires intention and consistency. It requires maintaining our promises, being there in their lives, and showing that their well-being is our top priority. It means creating a safe environment in which they can openly express their ideas and feelings without fear of being judged or rejected.

Children who trust their parents are more inclined to value and follow their counsel. They are also more likely to internalize their parents' values and beliefs, laying the groundwork for a faith-based and integrity-driven life.

Respect is another important aspect of a healthy parent-child relationship. It's a two-way street in which we respect each other's differences, value each other's viewpoints, and treat one another with kindness and consideration.

Parents demonstrate respect for their children by actively listening to their concerns, acknowledging their emotions, and incorporating them into family decisions. They refuse to undermine or criticize their children's beliefs and ideals, even if they differ from their own.

Children learn to respect their parents by observing their behavior, following their instructions, and respecting their boundaries. They learn that respect is earned by reciprocal love and consideration, not fear or intimidation.

When a family has mutual respect, communication flows effortlessly. Children feel safe sharing their thoughts and feelings because they know they will be heard and valued. Parents are confident in providing guidance and correction because they know their opinions will be received with open minds.

Open communication is crucial for any good connection, including parent-child relationships. Communication enables us to establish understanding, solve problems, and form connections.

Effective communication necessitates not only clear and honest speech, but also attentive and caring listening. It means taking the time to understand our children's ideas, even if we disagree with them, and communicating our own in a kind and productive manner.

When communication fails, misunderstandings emerge, resentment grows, and relationships deteriorate. However, when communication is robust, families may overcome challenges, celebrate successes, and grow closer together.

Recognizing the power of persistent love is also critical for creating the groundwork for discipline. Children must realize that their parents' affection is not based on their actions. They must be confident in the knowledge that they are loved for who they are, not just what they do.

This unconditional love fosters a safe environment in which youngsters can explore their surroundings, make mistakes, and learn from their experiences. It instills in people the courage to take risks, attempt new things, and reach their full potential.

Continuous love does not mean we forgo setting boundaries or punishing misconduct. It means we do so in a way that demonstrates our unwavering love and support, especially in the face of discipline.

It means offering our children hugs and encouraging words with criticism, reminding them that their mistakes do not diminish our love for them. It requires separating the behavior from the child and reinforcing their worthwhile confronting their actions.

Children who get regular love are more likely to respond favorably to discipline. They understand that correction is not a rejection, but rather a loving gesture designed to help them grow and learn.

This consistent love gives children a sense of security and belonging, which is essential for their emotional and spiritual development. When children feel secure in their parents' devotion, they are more prepared to face challenges, overcome disappointments, and develop a healthy sense of self-esteem.

Developing a strong foundation for discipline is an ongoing process that requires intentionality, consistency, and a lot of love. It is about prioritizing our relationships with our children and creating a safe and supportive atmosphere in which they can grow.

It is about communicating effectively, listening closely, and respecting their individuality. It is about continually demonstrating love and grace, especially in the face of rebuke, so that children understand they are cherished and treasured unconditionally.

When we lay this strong foundation, we create a fruitful climate for discipline to thrive and bear fruit. We encourage our children to accept criticism with open hearts, learn from their mistakes, and grow in wisdom and character.

Most importantly, we lay the groundwork for a lifelong and meaningful relationship with God.

Nurturing Connection and Trust

In the delicate ballet of parenting, where direction and love collide, the parent-child link is vital, serving as the foundation upon which all else is built. This sacred space encourages connection, builds trust, and sprouts seeds of faith.

A healthy parent-child connection is not merely a desirable outcome; it is an essential component of effective discipline. When children feel safe in their relationship with their parents, they are more receptive to direction, willing to cooperate, and more likely to internalize the values and beliefs taught.

Trust is the foundation of this relationship. It's the invisible thread that binds hearts together, offering a sense of safety and security. Children who trust their parents understand that they can rely on them for support, guidance, and unconditional love.

They feel at ease communicating their thoughts and feelings, knowing that they will be understood and appreciated.

Developing trust needs intentionality and consistency. It includes making ourselves physically and emotionally available to our children. It requires carefully listening to their concerns, recognizing their feelings, and responding with respect and compassion. It includes keeping our commitments, following through on them, and demonstrating that their well-being is our priority.

Honesty and transparency help to foster trust. When we are upfront and honest with our children about our challenges and vulnerabilities, we allow them to do the same. This vulnerability fosters a greater connection and allows them to see us as real people, not just authorities.

Respect is another key component of a healthy parent-child relationship. It is about recognizing everyone's inherent worth and dignity, regardless of age or ability. It means treating our children with the same kindness and consideration that we would give to anybody else, acknowledging their opinions, and respecting their boundaries.

Respectful parenting prevents harsh criticism, insulting words, and emotional manipulation. It means interacting calmly and politely with our children, including while disciplining them. It means acknowledging their feelings, even if we don't entirely understand them, and allowing them to express themselves without fear of being criticized.

When we respect our children, we educate them to value both themselves and others. We practice good communication habits and create an environment in which everyone feels respected and heard.

Open communication is vital for all healthy relationships, including the parent-child bond. It acts as a conduit for communication, dispute resolution, and mutual advancement.

Open communication requires both speaking and listening. It requires articulating our thoughts and feelings openly and honestly while remaining open to our children's viewpoints. It comprises asking questions, attempting to comprehend their experiences, and creating a secure environment for them to communicate their joys, anxieties, and concerns.

Active listening is an essential skill for promoting open conversation. It includes paying attention not only to the words said but also to underlying emotions and unspoken cues. To ensure comprehension, we must avoid distractions, maintain eye contact, and meditate on what we hear.

When we genuinely listen to our children, we are communicating that their thoughts and feelings are valuable. We build trust, strengthen relationships, and create an environment favorable to open and honest communication.

The regular rhythm of family life offers several opportunities to build connection and trust. **Here are some useful tips to consider:**

- Prioritize quality time. Set aside time every day to interact with your child, even if it's only for a few minutes. Participate in activities they enjoy, pay attention to their stories, and be completely present in those moments.

- Create shared experiences. Make time for family dinners, game nights, and group activities. These shared experiences help to create enduring memories and relationships.

- Show affection. You can communicate your love with words, embraces, or physical touch. Tell your child that they are loved and cherished.

- Offer encouragement. Celebrate their achievements, no matter how big or small, and offer words of encouragement at difficult times. Tell them you believe in their abilities and are proud of their accomplishments.

- Practice forgiveness. When conflict arises, as it inevitably does, be ready to forgive and seek settlement. Model humility and grace for your child, emphasizing the importance of relationships over being right.

- Pray together. Make prayer a regular part of your family practice. Pray for your child, pray with them, and teach them how to speak with God.

- Be a role model. Children learn by observing the adults in their lives. Model the behavior you want your children to display, such as honesty, respect, and kindness.

Nurturing connection and trust is an ongoing commitment that is built into the fabric of family life. It provides the foundation for effective discipline, encouraging children to grow, be resilient, and live lives of faith and purpose.

Unconditional Love in Action

Unconditional love is the foundation of a safe and nurturing environment in which children can develop. It is the unshakeable foundation upon which people build their understanding of themselves, their world, and their place within it. When children are bathed in unconditional love, they are free to explore, fall, and rise again, knowing that their value is not determined by their accomplishments or devotion to perfection.

This unconditional love promotes growth and learning, allowing children to reach their full potential without fear of judgment or rejection. It provides a safe environment in which children can experiment, make mistakes, and learn from their experiences while knowing that their parents' love is consistent and unchanging.

When children are disciplined in a loving environment, they are more likely to accept correction without feeling judged or rejected. They understand that their parent's disapproval of their actions does not diminish their feelings for them as individuals. This distinction is important because it helps youngsters understand that their worth is innate and not dependent on their behavior.

Unconditional love acts as a buffer, softening the severity of discipline and keeping it from becoming a source of shame or despair. It informs children that even if they make mistakes, they will be loved, valued, and accepted for who they are.

This sense of consistency is critical for a child's emotional and spiritual growth. When children feel secure in their parents' devotion, they are more prepared to face challenges, overcome disappointments, and develop a healthy sense of self-esteem. They are more likely to internalize their parents' values and guidance, not out of fear of punishment, but out of a desire to please those who love them unconditionally.

To demonstrate unconditional love amid punishment, you must be intentional and sensitive. It comprises utilizing words and actions to provide love and support, particularly when addressing wrongdoing. It requires distancing the youngster from their actions and praising them while correcting their mistakes.

Physical affection is a technique of expressing unconditional love. A warm hug, a gentle touch, or a reassuring pat on the back can express a lot of love and support, even during a disciplinary conversation. These physical gestures can help relieve stress, relax the child, and reinforce the message that they are unconditionally loved.

Verbal affirmations are another effective approach to communicating unconditional love. Statements like "I love you no matter what," "I'm proud of the person you are," or "I believe in you" can have a big impact on a kid's self-esteem and confidence. These affirmations should be delivered freely and lavishly throughout the parent-child relationship, not simply during disciplinary situations.

Active listening is another effective way to demonstrate love under punishment. Taking the time to truly hear and understand a child's point of view, especially if they have made a mistake, shows respect and empathy. It demonstrates the importance of their thoughts and feelings, even when their behaviors need to be corrected.

When we listen closely, we gain important insights into the motivations behind a child's behavior, allowing us to address the root causes rather than simply reacting to the symptoms. This strategy not only fosters understanding but also strengthens the parent-child bond by allowing for open and honest communication.

Another way to express unconditional love is to spend quality time together. Setting aside dedicated time to spend with our children, free of distractions or interruptions, provides a clear message about their value and importance in our lives. This quality time can take many forms, including reading books, playing games, having meaningful conversations, and sharing meals.

The goal is to give opportunities for connection and fun while making children feel seen, heard and appreciated. These moments of shared delight and laughter create positive memories and strengthen the emotional bond between parent and child, resulting in a reservoir of goodwill that can keep the relationship going even during difficult times.

Furthermore, demonstrating unconditional love requires modeling forgiveness. God forgives us freely and completely, and we must forgive our children when they make mistakes. This does not suggest supporting their behavior or rejecting the consequences of their actions; rather, it entails letting go of any hatred or anger and offering them a fresh start.

When we demonstrate forgiveness to our children, we teach them the importance of grace and reconciliation in their relationships with others and with God. We educate kids that mistakes are growth opportunities, and forgiveness leads to healing and restoration.

Unconditional love is the foundation of a secure and caring environment in which children can grow. It establishes a sense of acceptance and belonging, allowing children to make mistakes and learn from their experiences without fear of being criticized or rejected.

When discipline is used in the framework of unconditional love, it becomes a tool for growth and guidance, rather than a source of shame or discouragement. It teaches children that their worth is innate, not based on their actions, and that their parents' love persists even during correction.

By showing unconditional love via physical affection, vocal affirmations, active listening, quality time, and forgiveness, we provide a secure environment for our children to develop, learn, and form a deep and lasting connection with God.

Key Points

- → Trust is the foundation of a strong parent-child connection. Children need to know they can rely on you for regular affection and support.

- → Mutual respect is essential to efficient communication. Respecting one another's individuality and viewpoints develops a culture of understanding.

- → Open communication is vital for connecting and developing. It encourages free communication and effective conflict resolution.

- → Unconditional love provides a safe environment in which children can learn and grow. Knowing they are loved, regardless of their actions, gives them the confidence to succeed.

➡ It is vital to exhibit love while remaining disciplined. Affection, encouragement, and active listening all express affection, even when corrected.

Self-Reflection Questions

1. How do you demonstrate trustworthiness to your child? Are you consistent in both your words and actions? Do you fulfill your promises?

____

____

____

____

____

2. How do you respect your child's thoughts and feelings, even if they differ from your own?

____

____

____

____

3. How can you improve communication with your child? Are you allowing for open and honest dialogue?

____

____

____

____

4. How do you show your child unconditional love? Do your words and actions consistently communicate love, no matter how they behave?

____

____

____

____

____

5. How can you ensure that discipline is implemented in a loving and supportive environment? What specific steps can you take to ensure your child feels safe and respected, even during a correction?

____

____

____

____

____

Chapter 3: Setting Clear Expectations

"These commandments that I give you today are to be on your hearts. Impress them on your children. Talk about them when you sit at home and when you walk along the road, when you lie down and when you get up." Deuteronomy 6:6-7 (NIV)

This Deuteronomy verse depicts a faith-filled existence that extends beyond religious rites. It highlights parents' responsibility to teach God's commands in their children's minds and integrate them into their conversations, habits, and very being. This process begins with setting clear expectations, establishing boundaries that reflect God's values, and encouraging children to a healthy lifestyle.

Setting clear expectations for our children is analogous to presenting a blueprint; it helps them comprehend the road they should take and the boundaries that will keep them safe. It is about explaining what is acceptable and unacceptable, right and wrong, in a clear, consistent, and age-appropriate way.

When young people understand what is expected of them, they are less likely to veer from their path. They feel safe because they understand the boundaries and are empowered to make sound decisions that are in line with their family's values and God's laws.

Clear expectations provide a framework for discipline. When children understand the rules and the consequences of breaking them, discipline turns away from arbitrary punishment and toward natural consequences and opportunities for growth.

Setting clear expectations is not a one-size-fits-all approach. It is critical to consider the child's age, developmental stage, and unique needs. What is appropriate for a toddler may not be what is expected of a teenager.

For younger children, expectations may need to be simple and concrete, with a focus on core behaviors like sharing, listening, and respecting others. As children get older, their expectations may become more sophisticated, incorporating values such as honesty, accountability, and self-control.

The idea is to explain expectations in terms that youngsters may easily understand. Avoid using unclear language or confusing standards that allow for interpretation. Instead, use explicit and plain language to communicate what is required.

Instead of saying "Be good," which is subjective and vague, say "Use kind words when talking to your brother" or "Put your toys away when you're finished playing." This customized language removes doubt and helps children understand what is expected of them.

Consistency is vital for setting clear expectations. Children thrive on structure and routine. When expectations are uneven or constantly changing, children get confused and insecure. They may test boundaries more frequently, causing power struggles and dissatisfaction for both parents and children.

Consistency requires following the rules fairly and consistently, regardless of the situation or our attitude. It requires acting on consequences when expectations are not realized, even if they are challenging or unpleasant.

This constancy increases children's sense of stability and security. They learn to trust their parents' words and anticipate predictable outcomes from their actions. This consistency instills in children a sense of responsibility and accountability, allowing them to develop self-control and make wise judgments.

While clear expectations and strict enforcement are essential, effective communication is also required. To effectively communicate expectations, we must not only say what we mean but also how we express it. It requires us to be conscious of our tone of voice, body language, and general mood.

When addressing expectations, keep a calm and courteous demeanor. Avoid yelling, lecturing, or using harsh language. Instead, speak plainly and directly, maintaining eye contact and conveying your point with firmness and kindness.

Body language is a crucial part of communication. Maintain an open and friendly approach while avoiding crossed arms and serious faces. Use gestures and facial expressions to reinforce your words and make your point clear.

Active listening is another key component of effective communication. Take the time to hear and understand your child's point of view, even if they disagree with your expectations or have broken the rules. This active listening demonstrates respect and empathy, facilitating open communication and understanding.

When children feel heard and understood, they are more willing to cooperate and meet expectations. They are also more inclined to adopt the ideas and ideals that underpin the rules, making them their own rather than simply obeying them out of fear of punishment.

Additionally, successful communication necessitates clear and explicit explanations. Do not assume that children understand the reasons for your expectations or the consequences of their behavior. Take the time to explain why specific behaviors are essential, how they affect others, and how they align with your family's beliefs and God's rules.

This explanation helps children understand that your demands are not arbitrary or controlling, but rather motivated by love, wisdom, and concern for their well-being. It also helps youngsters to make educated choices and take responsibility for their actions.

Finally, remember that creating clear expectations is an ongoing process, not a one-time event. As children mature, their understanding of the world expands, as does their ability to manage responsibility. Parents must regularly review and adjust expectations to ensure that they are age-appropriate and relevant to their child's developmental stage.

This ongoing process may include examining family norms, discussing new issues, and empowering children to help set their own goals and expectations. This collaborative approach fosters a sense of ownership and responsibility, enabling children to actively participate in their growth and development.

Setting clear expectations is vital for developing God-fearing children. It acts as a guidepost for their actions, a framework for discipline, and the foundation for their understanding of God's laws.

We create a safe and supportive environment for children to grow by communicating expectations, consistently, and respectfully. We help youngsters make sound decisions, accept responsibility for their actions, and develop intelligence and character.

Most importantly, we provide the groundwork for a life that honors God, reflects His values, and glorifies Him.

Establishing Age-Appropriate Boundaries

Children are not miniature adults; they have distinct needs, abilities, and developmental stages that must be carefully considered while establishing limits and expectations. What is appropriate for a teenager could be overwhelming or even harmful for a toddler. As a result, we must tailor our punishment and guidance to the child's age and level of understanding.

Children spend their early years, from infancy to preschool, exploring their surroundings, developing their senses, and establishing a sense of safety. Boundaries during this period should be centered on safety, basic routines, and simple social interactions.

Establishing a consistent bedtime routine, for example, helps regulate a child's sleep habits and promotes predictability. Teaching youngsters how to share toys and take turns fosters social skills and collaboration. Setting limits on physical aggression, such as hitting or biting, teaches children the importance of respecting others.

As children enter elementary school, their cognitive abilities grow, and they become more capable of understanding abstract notions like fairness and accountability. During this stage, boundaries can be established to promote self-control, property respect, and accountability.

This could involve limiting screen time, assigning tasks around the house, or defining criteria for completing assignments. It also teaches children to be honest, apologize when they make errors, and consider the consequences of their actions.

Adolescents struggle with identity formation, independence, and heightened awareness of societal factors. During this stage, boundaries should be established to promote accountability, good decision-making, and navigating challenging social situations.

Curfews, dating and social media guidelines, and encouraging open discussion about peer pressure and risky behavior are all solutions. It also means allowing youngsters to develop their independence while providing adequate parental guidance and support.

Expectations should be conveyed clearly and simply at all stages of development. Children must understand what is expected of them in an age-appropriate and straightforward manner. Avoid employing unclear terminology or complex rules that they may struggle to understand.

For example, instead of just saying "Behave yourself," which is subjective and open to interpretation, give specific instructions like "Use kind words when speaking to your sister" or "Wait your turn before speaking."

When setting limitations, it is critical to give clear and consistent penalties for misconduct. These sanctions should be proportionate to the offense and appropriate for the child's age and understanding.

For a tiny child, tossing a toy may result in the toy being taken away for a brief period. For an older child, failing to complete tasks may result in a loss of privileges, such as screen time or a planned outing.

The purpose of consequences is not to punish or harm children, but rather to help them understand the natural consequences of their actions and motivate them to make better decisions in the future. It is about teaching kids responsibility, accountability, and the importance of conforming their behavior to their family's values and God's commands.

When establishing limits and expectations, it is critical to achieve a balance of firmness and flexibility. While consistency is essential, it is also important to recognize that each child is an individual with distinct needs and experiences.

There may be times when it is appropriate to adjust expectations or make exceptions based on a child's specific situation. For example, a child suffering from anxiety or a learning disability may require different boundaries or support than a child who does not have these issues.

This flexibility demonstrates empathy and compassion while maintaining the overall structure and stability that children require to thrive. It also encourages open communication and teamwork since children feel comfortable expressing their needs and concerns without fear of being judged or rejected.

Setting age-appropriate limits is a continual process that requires patience, wisdom, and a willingness to adapt as children grow and mature. It's about providing kids with the structure and guidance they need to thrive while also celebrating their individuality and supporting their freedom.

We establish a safe and caring environment for children to learn self-control, make good decisions, and grow in their relationship with God by setting clear expectations, communicating them effectively, and constantly enforcing them.

<u>**Communicating Effectively with Your Child**</u>

Communication is the basis of all healthy relationships, including the parent-child link. It connects hearts, minds, and spirits, facilitating understanding, growth, and mutual respect. When families communicate openly, they can overcome problems, celebrate accomplishments, and grow closer.

Establishing clear expectations necessitates effective communication. It is not enough to simply establish rules and boundaries; we must also communicate those expectations to our children in a way that is clear, consistent, and understandable.

Effective communication with children needs a comprehensive plan that includes not only what we say, but also how we listen, the tone we use, and how consistently we follow through.

Active listening is an essential component of excellent communication. To properly listen to our children, we must pay attention to their nonverbal cues, comprehend their underlying emotions, and respect their viewpoints.

Active listening necessitates putting aside our own thoughts and agendas, as well as any mental clutter that may impede us from hearing what our children are saying. It requires giving them our undivided attention, creating eye contact, and using body language to express our interest and involvement.

When we listen carefully, we create a safe environment in which our children may express themselves honestly and openly. We teach children that their thoughts and feelings matter, even if they differ from ours. This affirmation fosters trust and respect, laying the groundwork for a constructive and communicative connection.

Active listening allows us to better grasp our children's motivations, worries, and desires. It helps us understand the "why" behind their behavior, allowing us to treat the root causes rather than just the symptoms.

For example, if a child repeatedly refuses to go to bed, active listening could indicate an underlying fear of the dark or a need for more touch with their parents. Understanding these underlying needs enables us to meet them with understanding and compassion, yielding solutions that benefit both the parent and the child.

Another crucial part of efficient communication is to use clear and accurate language. Children, especially younger ones, may struggle to comprehend complex language or abstract concepts. When discussing expectations, use plain, direct language that they will comprehend.

Avoid using imprecise phrases like "be good" or "behave yourself," as they are open to interpretation and may not provide specific instructions. Instead, use plain, detailed language to communicate what is expected.

Instead of repeating the phrase "Don't make a mess," specify "Please put your toys away when you're finished playing" as well as "Remember to wipe up any spills." This customized language removes doubt and helps children understand what is expected of them.

Consistency in our communication is equally important. Children thrive on structure and routine. When our words and actions align, people learn to trust our advice and understand that our expectations are firm and consistent.

This homogeneity extends to both our vocal and nonverbal communication. If we say one thing but our body language or tone of voice conveys a different message, children may become confused or distrustful. For example, if we tell a child to clean up their room while sighing and rolling our eyes, they may take the request as phony or trivial.

Consistency also refers to meeting our expectations. If we make a rule but do not consistently enforce it, children may assume that our remarks are not to be taken seriously. They may test boundaries more frequently, causing power struggles and dissatisfaction for both parents and children.

Following through on our expectations means applying the rules fairly and consistently, regardless of the situation or our attitude. It comprises implementing consequences for failing to meet expectations, even if they are harsh or unpleasant.

This constancy increases children's sense of stability and security. They learn to trust their parents' words and anticipate predictable outcomes from their actions. This consistency instills in children a sense of responsibility and accountability, allowing them to develop self-control and make wise judgments.

Allowing for debate and feedback is another part of effective communication. Don't just lecture your children; instead, involve them in discussions about expectations, rules, and consequences. Ask them questions to ensure their understanding, and encourage them to express their thoughts and feelings.

This open communication not only fosters understanding but also teaches children to take responsibility for their actions. It shows that their opinions are valued and that children have a voice in the home.

When engaging with your children, keep your emotions under check. If you're angry, frustrated, or anxious, take a moment to calm down before beginning a disciplinary conversation. Strong emotions may compromise our judgment, resulting in harsh, reactive, or inconsistent communications.

When you approach your child in a calm and attentive manner, you create a better environment for conversation. You are better able to articulate your expectations clearly, listen empathetically, and reply with wisdom and grace.

Key Points

→ Clear expectations provide a road map for children's behavior. They set boundaries and help children make sensible decisions.

→ Expectations should be age-appropriate and tailored to each individual's requirements. A child is supposed to behave differently than a teenager.

→ Communicate your expectations in clear and straightforward language. Avoid unclear terminology and instead provide explicit, direct instructions.

→ Consistency is critical for instilling a sense of security and predictability. Enforce regulations fairly and consistently, regardless of the circumstances.

→ Active listening and clear explanations are critical components of successful communication. Spend time understanding your child's point of view and explaining why you have specific expectations.

1. Are your expectations for your child clear, specific, and age-appropriate? How do you make things more concrete and understandable?

2. How do you continuously enforce your expectations? Do you follow through on consequences, even if they are inconvenient?

3. How well do you listen to your child's point of view, even when they've broken the rules?

4. How well do you convey the rationale behind your expectations? Does your child understand why certain habits are important?

____

____

____

____

____

5. How can you improve your communication with your child to promote more understanding and cooperation?

____

____

____

____

____

Chapter 4: Responding to Misbehavior

This proverb acknowledges a fact that all parents are well aware of: children are intrinsically prone to make mistakes. Their hearts, while full of wonder and possibility, are nevertheless prone to foolishness and poor judgment. Discipline, portrayed here as the "rod," is critical in leading children away from these hazards and toward a path of wisdom and morality.

Responding to disobedience is an unavoidable part of parenting. No matter how well we prepare, how we convey expectations, or how lovingly we nurture our children, they will periodically stray from the road, make poor decisions, or push the boundaries. These scenarios can be stressful, annoying, and sometimes depressing for parents.

However, it is vital to recognize that misbehavior is more than just disobedience or a deliberate attempt to cause trouble. It is frequently a cry for help, signaling that something more serious is going on in a child's heart or head.

Rather than reacting in hatred or fury, we are taught to respond with wisdom, discernment, and empathy. We are required to delve behind the surface, understand the root causes of disobedience, and respond with compassion and instruction.

Identifying the source of the problem is the first step in responding appropriately to misbehavior. This urges us to put aside our prejudices and preconceptions and approach our children with inquiry and empathy. It requires asking probing questions, paying close attention, and trying to understand their point of view.

Sometimes the cause of misbehavior is evident. A youngster may act out because they are tired, hungry, or overstimulated. They may be struggling with a new situation, like starting school or adjusting to a shift in family dynamics.

Sometimes the underlying cause is unclear. A child may misbehave to get attention, challenge boundaries, or express underlying emotions such as annoyance, concern, or despair. They may be experiencing peer pressure, academic difficulties, or feelings of inadequacy.

By taking the time to understand the underlying causes of misbehavior, we may tailor our response to our child's specific needs. We can offer assistance, guidance, and encouragement as they manage challenges and develop healthy coping strategies.

For example, if a child is acting out due to stress or concern, we may help them identify and manage their emotions, teach them relaxation techniques, and create a quiet environment at home. If a child misbehaves for attention, we can respond with positive attention and affirmation, making them feel recognized and loved.

Identifying the root cause of misconduct allows us to differentiate between willful disobedience and unintentional mistakes. Children are not perfect, and they will inevitably make mistakes as they learn and grow. These mistakes should be considered as opportunities for learning and growth, rather than as justification for harsh punishment or condemnation.

When a child makes a mistake, it is vital to respond with compassion and grace. Help them understand the consequences of their acts, guide them toward making apologies, and encourage them to make better decisions in the future.

However, when a child actively disobeys or deliberately chooses to ignore expectations, a different approach may be required. In these circumstances, it is vital to address the defiance directly, set clear boundaries, and enforce consistent consequences.

The goal is not to punish the child but to teach them the importance of respecting authority, following rules, and taking responsibility for their actions. It is about teaching youngsters that their choices have consequences and that they are accountable for their actions.

When dealing with misbehavior, it is vital to employ disciplinary tools and techniques that are in line with biblical ideals and promote connection. This involves avoiding methods that are harsh, punishing, or humiliating. Instead, we should use firm, caring, and instructional techniques.

Natural consequences are an effective disciplinary strategy. Natural repercussions are the direct results of a child's actions. For example, if a toddler refuses to eat dinner, they will undoubtedly be hungry later. If children fail to accomplish their obligations, their rooms will undoubtedly get disorganized.

Natural consequences are an excellent learning opportunity for children because they help them understand the relationship between their actions and the results. They also teach young people responsibility and accountability by making them aware of the consequences of their actions.

Another effective strategy is logical consequences. Parents enforce rational consequences that are directly related to misbehavior. For example, if a child breaks a toy, the natural outcome may be that they lose the privilege to play with that toy for some time. If they mistreat a sibling, the natural consequence may be that they must spend time alone in their room.

Logical consequences should be clear, consistent, and proportionate to the offense. They should also be communicated to the child in a way that helps them understand the link between their behavior and the consequences.

In addition to natural and logical consequences, additional disciplinary tactics can be effective when used effectively. Time-outs are a brief period of separation that can help a child relax and regain control. Loss of privileges may motivate a child to change their behavior by temporarily taking away what they value.

However, it is critical to note that these tactics should be used rarely and cautiously. The goal is not to punish the child, but to assist them make better choices and accept responsibility for their actions.

When dealing with wrongdoing, it is vital to maintain calm and control. Avoid expressing anger or frustration, as this may aggravate the problem and deepen the distance between you and your child.

Instead, take some time to gather your thoughts, pray for wisdom and guidance, and then approach your child with compassion and understanding. Speak clearly and firmly while demonstrating love and compassion.

Understanding the Roots of Misbehavior

Children are complex beings, full of emotions, desires, and developing knowledge. Their conduct, like a reflection in a pool of water, is influenced by a variety of internal and external factors. When misbehavior happens, it is common to react immediately, addressing the surface-level acts without considering the underlying currents that may be motivating them. To effectively support our children's growth and maturity, we must look below the surface, attempting to understand the root causes of their misbehavior.

This knowing process requires parents to take a curious and empathy-filled approach, considering their children as individuals to be understood rather than adversaries to be subjugated. It requires setting aside our assumptions and judgments and approaching them with a genuine desire to see the world through their eyes.

One of the first steps in determining the causes of misbehavior is to determine the child's developmental stage. Children of varying ages have unique abilities, needs, and perspectives on the world. Throwing a tantrum or refusing to share may be considered misbehavior in a toddler, but it could also be perfectly normal for their developmental stage.

Children's cognitive and emotional abilities expand, as does their understanding of social standards and expectations. What is considered rebellion in a teenager, such as opposing authority or pushing limits, may be a normal part of their drive for independence and identity.

Understanding the developmental milestones and challenges associated with each stage of life can provide valuable insights into the motivations motivating a child's behavior. We can respond with greater empathy and employ disciplinary measures that are appropriate for their age and level of comprehension.

Another crucial factor to consider is the child's temperament and personality. Every child is unique, with own strengths, weaknesses, and sensitivities. Some children are naturally more outgoing and spontaneous, while others are more reserved and cautious. Some are highly sensitive to sensory input, while others are more adaptable and easygoing.

These individual differences can have a significant impact on how children react to situations and express their emotions. A naturally sensitive child may react more intensely to perceived criticism or frustration, whereas an impulsive child may struggle with self-control and act out unconsciously.

Recognizing and accepting our children's temperaments enables us to tailor our parenting strategies to their distinct needs. We may provide more support to those who are more sensitive, set clear boundaries for those who are more impulsive, and create an environment in which each child may develop in their unique way.

External effects must be addressed with developmental and individual traits. Children are constantly bombarded with messages and stimuli from their environment, including television and social media, peer connections, and cultural expectations. These external circumstances can significantly influence their ideas, attitudes, and behaviors.

For example, if the child is exposed to violent media or witnesses aggressive behavior among their peers, they may be more likely to engage in the same behaviors themselves. If adolescents are constantly assaulted with messages about material possessions or popularity, they may develop unhealthy priorities or feelings of inadequacy.

As parents, we must be mindful of the external elements that influence our children's hearts and minds. We must be proactive in filtering out bad messages, establishing positive examples, and creating a home environment that aligns with our values and aims.

Furthermore, we must acknowledge the importance of unfulfilled needs in misbehavior. Children, like all humans, have basic needs for love, security, belonging, and importance. When these desires are not met, people may act out to satisfy them.

For example, a youngster who feels neglected or undesired may act out to gain attention, even if it is unpleasant. A child who is insecure or scared may cling to or refuse separation from their parents. A young person who feels weak or insignificant may try to assert authority through defiance or hostility.

Recognizing unmet needs enables us to respond with compassion and empathy. We may show our children more love and attention, provide a more stable and predictable environment, and allow them to feel respected and powerful.

Finally, remember that misbehavior does not always indicate a serious ailment. Sometimes it's just a normal part of growing up, a reflection of a child's developing brain and ongoing quest to comprehend their surroundings.

Children are inherently curious and exploring. As they learn and mature, they will test their limits and make mistakes. These experiences are not necessarily indicative of a larger problem, but rather an expected part of their development.

When dealing with this type of misconduct, it is vital to maintain a balanced perspective. Don't overreact or label your child as "bad" or "troubled." Instead, focus on guiding them, setting clear expectations, and allowing them to learn from their failures.

<u>**Disciplinary Tools and Techniques**</u>

Disciplining children in a way that honors God and supports their growth demands a toolbox full of diverse and adaptable strategies. It's about understanding the nuances of each tool, choosing the right one for the job, and applying it with wisdom, compassion, and discretion.

Natural consequences are one of the most effective tactics a parent can use. These are the natural repercussions of a child's behavior, with no intervention from the parent. For example, if a child refuses to wear a coat on a chilly day, they will undoubtedly be cold. If students fail to complete their homework, they may receive a worse grade or miss out on a fun activity.

Natural consequences give valuable learning opportunities for children by highlighting the direct relationship between their actions and the results. They teach children responsibility and accountability, demonstrating that their actions have real-world repercussions.

However, it is vital to use natural consequences responsibly. When a child's safety or well-being is compromised, natural consequences may not be suitable. For example, if a toddler rushes into the street without looking, the natural consequence could be disastrous. In these cases, active intervention and clear boundaries are essential to protect the child from harm.

When natural consequences are neither possible nor safe, logical consequences can be a viable alternative. Parents enforce rational consequences that are directly related to misbehavior. For example, if a child destroys a toy out of carelessness, the obvious consequence could be that they lose the privilege of playing with that thing for an extended length of time. If they speak disrespectfully to a family member, they may need to spend some time alone in their room to reflect on their conduct.

Logical consequences should be clear, consistent, and proportionate to the offense. They should also be communicated to the child in a way that helps them understand the link between their behavior and the consequences. The goal isn't to punish the child but to help them learn from their mistakes and make better decisions in the future.

A time-out is another effective form of discipline. Time-outs provide a temporary respite from the hectic environment, allowing a child to unwind, regain self-control, and reflect on their behavior. This can be especially helpful for younger children, who are frequently overwhelmed by strong emotions.

Time-outs should be administered calmly and regularly. Choose a serene, distraction-free environment. The duration of the time-out should be appropriate for the child's age and developmental stage, typically one minute each year of age.

Avoid engaging or lecturing the child during the time out. The purpose is to provide a break from the conflict, not to worsen it. Following the timeout, calmly discuss the misbehavior with the child, emphasizing why it was wrong and how to make better decisions in the future.

When used correctly, loss of privileges can be a useful disciplinary tool. This involves temporarily taking away something the child values, like screen time, a cherished toy, or an anticipated outing. The loss of privilege should be directly related to the wrongdoing and implemented consistently.

It is vital to explain to the youngsters why they are losing the privilege and how they might retrieve it by positive behavior. This technique teaches children that their actions have repercussions and that they may make choices that lead to positive outcomes.

In addition to these specific tactics, other strategies can be effective in dealing with misbehavior. Redirection can benefit young children by diverting their attention away from disruptive conduct and toward a more acceptable activity. For example, if a child is hurling toys, redirect them to a coloring book or a block activity.

Excellent reinforcement is another powerful way to encourage good behavior and motivate children to make sound decisions. Praise, encouragement, and prizes can be used to acknowledge and reward a child's efforts and accomplishments.

However, positive reinforcement should be utilized cautiously. Overuse of rewards can lead to a youngster becoming reliant on external affirmation, decreasing their inner desire. The goal is to help children develop a sense of internal satisfaction and pride in their accomplishments rather than simply motivating them with external rewards.

Finally, the most effective disciplinary method is one tailored to each child and the specific situation. What works for one youngster may not work for another. What is appropriate in one setting could be inappropriate in another.

As parents, we must be attentive to our children's needs, observant of their behavior, and willing to adapt our approach as they grow and mature. We must be judicious in our use of disciplinary tools, employing them with wisdom, love, and a desire to foster connection and progress.

Key Points

→ Misbehavior is frequently an indication that something more serious is going on. It is necessary to go under the surface and find the root causes.

→ Identifying the root cause of misbehavior permits a more effective response. Addressing underlying needs can assist in preventing such incidents.

→ Natural and logical consequences are useful teaching tools. They help children grasp the relationship between their actions and the outcomes.

→ Time-outs and loss of privileges can be useful when used properly. They should be carried out quietly, consistently, and with clear instructions.

→ Discipline should be done with compassion and firmness, not fury or impatience. The goal is to advise and educate, not punish or disgrace.

Self-Reflection Questions

1. How do you normally deal with your child's misbehavior? Do you reply in the moment or do you take your time evaluating the situation?

____

____

____

____

____

2. How good are you at identifying the root causes of your child's misbehavior? What steps can you take to improve your understanding?

____

____

____

____

____

3. Which disciplinary tools and processes do you find most effective? Are they consistent with Christian values and build relationships with your child?

____

____

____

____

____

4. How can you remain cool and controlled while your youngster misbehaves? What tactics can you use to control your own emotions?

____

____

____

____

____

5. How do you ensure that your disciplinary approach is targeted at guiding and teaching your child, rather than simply punishing?

____

____

____

Chapter 5: Guiding with Grace

"Therefore, as God's chosen people, holy and dearly loved, clothe yourselves with compassion, kindness, humility, gentleness and patience. Bear with each other and forgive one another if any of you has a grievance against someone. Forgive as the Lord forgave you." Colossians 3:12-13 (NIV)

This verse from Colossians nicely portrays what it means to live as God's people, with attributes that reflect His character. It inspires us to be compassionate, kind, humble, gentle, and patient toward one another, culminating in the great act of forgiveness. These characteristics are more than just ideals for peaceful living; they are the essence of God's grace in action, and they serve as the foundation for lovingly disciplining our children.

Guiding with grace includes viewing discipline not as a punishment, but as an opportunity for growth, healing, and deeper connection. It includes accepting that our children, like all of us, are flawed and prone to making mistakes. It requires treating their mistakes with respect, compassion, and a willingness to forgive.

Grace is not about lowering standards or excusing wrongdoing. It is about acknowledging that our children are on a journey of learning and development and that mistakes are an inescapable part of that process. It is about showing them the same unconditional love and forgiveness that God extends to us.

When we discipline with grace, we foster an environment in which our children feel comfortable acknowledging their errors, seeking our guidance, and learning from their mistakes. We show them that our love for them is not dependent on their actions and that our acceptance of them is not based on their perfection.

This unconditional love and acceptance provides a solid foundation for children's growth and maturity. They learn that even when they fall short, they are still valued, appreciated, and beloved. This understanding enables children to take risks, try new things, and face challenges with confidence, knowing that their parents will always be there to support them.

One of the most powerful ways to demonstrate grace is to stress forgiveness. Forgiveness is more than simply letting go of anger or resentment; it is an intentional decision to free someone from the debt they owe us, to give them a new beginning, and to move forward in a relationship.

When we forgive our children, we demonstrate God's heart, which freely forgives our mistakes and gives us a fresh start through Christ. We show that mistakes do not define people and that their past actions do not determine their future.

Forgiveness promotes reconciliation and healing. When we forgive our children, we provide an opportunity to rebuild trust, strengthen our bonds, and go forward in love and peace.

The path to forgiveness and healing is not always easy. It may require us to lay aside our bitter feelings, recognize our involvement in the disagreement, and demonstrate grace even when we sense it is undeserved.

However, the advantages of forgiveness are great. It frees us from bitterness and resentment, which can poison our emotions and damage our relationships. It allows us to experience God's healing power while simultaneously offering that grace to our children.

In addition to forgiving our children, we must teach them to forgive themselves. Children can be quite hard on themselves, carrying the weight of their mistakes even after we have forgiven them. They may feel guilt, shame, or inadequacy, believing that their actions have irrevocably harmed their relationship with their parents or God.

We can help our children forgive themselves by reminding them of God's unconditional love and forgiveness. We can comfort them that their mistakes do not define them and that their past actions do not determine their future.

We can also encourage them to confess their faults to God, seek His forgiveness, and trust in His grace to fix them. This process of confession and repentance may be immensely liberating for children, freeing them from the load of guilt and shame and helping them to move on with confidence and optimism.

Guiding with grace means showing humility and contrition in our own lives. As parents, we are not perfect. We make mistakes, lose patience, and say or do things we come to regret.

When these situations arise, we must acknowledge our mistakes, apologize to our children, and seek their forgiveness. This vulnerability can be uncomfortable, but it is incredibly useful to our children.

It illustrates that we are not flawless, that we make mistakes just like they do, and that we are willing to accept responsibility for our actions. This sincerity develops a greater sense of trust and connection, allowing our children to see us as genuine people eager to grow and learn alongside them.

When we admit our flaws, we must do it with honesty and humility. Avoid making excuses or blaming others. Instead, accept responsibility for your behavior and sincerely apologize for whatever suffering you have caused.

You may say, "I'm sorry I yelled at you earlier." I was frustrated, but that wasn't an excuse for responding to you that way. "Will you forgive me?"

The simple act of admitting your mistake and begging for forgiveness can have a big impact on your child. It teaches kids the value of humility, accountability, and reconciliation. It also teaches children that even adults make mistakes and that it is okay to ask for forgiveness.

In addition to confessing our sins, we can show repentance by actively seeking to make amends. This may include apologizing to our child for our faults, offering to make things right, or changing our behavior in the future.

For example, if you have frequently criticized your child's efforts, you may apologize and resolve to be more encouraging and supportive. If you've been disregarding your child's need for attention, you may make a serious effort to spend more quality time with them.

These behaviors demonstrate that repentance requires more than just words. It indicates to our children that we really apologize for our mistakes and are determined to change our behavior.

Furthermore, modeling humility and repentance requires acknowledging our own need for God's favor. We are all flawed creatures who make mistakes and fall short of God's standards. We need His forgiveness, guidance, and ability to walk in righteousness.

When we publicly acknowledge our need for God, we teach our children the importance of humility and trusting in God's grace. We teach children that even adults need God's help and that it is okay to seek His forgiveness and guidance.

This openness can also improve spiritual interactions with our children. We can discuss our challenges and triumphs, as well as our experiences with God's love and forgiveness. We can encourage them to seek God's guidance in their own lives, confess their sins, and trust in His help to overcome problems.

When we guide our children with grace, we not only correctly discipline them, but we also direct them to the ultimate source of grace, the One who offers forgiveness, healing, and a new beginning to all who seek Him.

The Power of Forgiveness

In the complicated dance of parenting, when mistakes and misunderstandings are unavoidable, forgiveness emerges as a guiding light, illuminating the path to healing, reconciliation, and renewed connection. It is the balm that heals wounded hearts, the bridge that mends broken relationships, and the catalyst that encourages growth and transformation.

Forgiveness, in its most basic form, is the act of releasing resentment, rage, or hurt toward someone who has harmed us. It is a conscious decision to reject the desire for vengeance or retribution in favor of kindness and compassion.

In the context of discipline, forgiveness is essential for restoring harmony and developing a positive parent-child connection. When children misbehave, it's easy to get caught up in the moment and become angry, annoyed, or disappointed. However, allowing these emotions to fester can create barriers between us and our children, impeding communication and progress.

Forgiveness, on the other hand, allows us to get beyond the offense, see our children through the lens of compassion, and respond with love and understanding. It creates an environment in which mistakes are recognized as opportunities for growth, reconciliation is valued, and relationships flourish.

Forgiveness is not about tolerating wrongdoing or pretending it did not happen. It is about acknowledging the harm or injury done but also understanding that our children are imperfect beings who, like us, are capable of making mistakes.

When we forgive our children, we lift their burden of guilt and humiliation, allowing them to begin again with a fresh slate. We convey our unconditional love for them, emphasizing that they are cherished and welcomed regardless of their actions.

This unconditional love and acceptance creates a safe environment in which children can develop and learn. They feel secure knowing that their parents' love will never be broken and that they can make mistakes without fear of rejection or condemnation. This security fosters trust and openness, allowing young people to take risks, try new things, and learn from their experiences without fear of failure.

Forgiveness is something we not only give to our children but also expect from them. As parents, we are not perfect. We will make mistakes, lose patience, and say things we later regret. In such cases, it is necessary to humble ourselves, recognize our flaws, and ask our children for forgiveness.

This act of humility teaches our children the importance of taking responsibility for our actions and seeking forgiveness when we have injured others. It also strengthens our bond with them by demonstrating that we value their forgiveness and are determined to maintain a healthy and respectful relationship.

Both parents and children may struggle to forgive and be forgiven. It requires vulnerability, humility, and a willingness to let go of pain and bitterness. However, the advantages of forgiveness are great.

When forgiveness becomes a regular practice in our households, we create a culture of grace and compassion. It fosters an environment in which mistakes are recognized as opportunities for growth, relationships are prioritized above pride, and love and connection are key.

Here are some practical strategies to offer and accept forgiveness during the punishment process:

For Parents:

→ Recognize your own emotions. When your child misbehaves, take the time to recognize and manage your feelings. This allows you to respond with clarity and compassion, rather than rage or impatience.

→ Separate the behavior from the child. Remember, your child's misbehavior does not define them. Affirm their worth and value while addressing their behavior.

→ Communicate your forgiveness. To express your forgiveness openly, use phrases like "I forgive you" or "I'm not angry anymore".

➜ Make a fresh start. Tell your child that you are moving forward and will not hold their mistake against them.

➜ Model forgiveness in your relationships. Show your children forgiveness through your interactions with your spouse, family members, and friends.

For Children:

➜ Help them understand what forgiveness implies. Explain that forgiveness does not imply forgetting or excusing wrongdoing, but rather choosing to let go of wrath and resentment.

➜ Encourage them to express their feelings. Create a safe space for them to vent their hurt or anger, and help them healthily process their feelings.

➜ Help them accept responsibility for their actions. Help them understand the implications of their actions and encourage them to make amends wherever possible.

➜ Teach them how to ask for forgiveness. Show how to apologize and beg forgiveness from people whom they have wronged.

➜ Help them comprehend the importance of self-forgiveness. Encourage them to let go of their guilt and shame, and instead go on with confidence and grace.

As we guide our children with grace, remember that we are reflecting the heart of our Heavenly Father, who offers us forgiveness and a fresh start every day. May we show our children the same grace, making our home a place of love, forgiveness, and reconciliation.

Modeling Humility and Repentance

In the delicate dance of parenting, when we try to guide our children toward a life of faith and righteousness, it's easy to fall into the trap of adopting a perfectionist attitude. We may believe that as parents, we must always have the answers, make sound decisions, and offer a good example of virtue and wisdom.

However, chasing parental perfection is both impossible and detrimental. It imposes an unattainable norm, which may make us feel inadequate and discouraged. It can also impede our children's development since they may struggle to relate to a parent who appears to be perfect and incapable of making mistakes.

Instead of striving for the illusion of perfection, we are taught to recognize the power of humility and remorse. These attributes, which are sometimes interpreted as signs of weakness in our culture, are indicators of genuine faith and leadership.

Humility allows us to understand our limitations, accept our mistakes, and acknowledge that we are all on a journey of learning and progress. It frees us from the need to be perfect and allows us to truly connect with our children.

When we model humility, we create a safe environment in which our children can acknowledge their own mistakes, seek forgiveness, and grow in grace. We teach youngsters that it is okay to make mistakes as long as we learn from them and strive to improve in the future.

Repentance goes hand in hand with humility. It is the act of turning away from our mistakes and attempting to make amends to people we have wronged. It is about acknowledging the repercussions of our actions and taking responsibility for our choices.

When we model repentance, we teach our children the importance of accepting responsibility for their mistakes, seeking forgiveness from those they have hurt, and apologizing for their acts. We show them that repentance is not a sign of weakness, but rather a way to heal and restore.

Recognizing our faults is one of the most effective methods to teach our children humility and repentance. This could include confessing when we've been impatient, unfair, or careless. It may mean confessing when we have spoken harshly, acted in wrath, or made a decision that has injured our child.

These admissions may seem awkward or even vulnerable, yet they are tremendously useful to our children. They show us that we are not perfect, that we make mistakes just like them, and that we are willing to accept responsibility for our actions.

This sincerity promotes a greater sense of trust and connection. It allows our children to see us as genuine people with flaws and foibles who are trying to grow and learn with them.

When we admit our flaws, we must do it with honesty and humility. Avoid making excuses or blaming others. Instead, accept responsibility for your behavior and sincerely apologize for whatever suffering you have caused.

You may say, "I'm sorry I yelled at you earlier." I was frustrated, but that wasn't an excuse for responding to you that way. "Will you forgive me?"

The simple act of admitting your mistake and begging for forgiveness can have a big impact on your child. It teaches kids the value of humility, accountability, and reconciliation. It also teaches children that even adults make mistakes and that it is okay to ask for forgiveness.

In addition to confessing our sins, we can show repentance by actively seeking to make amends. This may include apologizing to our child for our faults, offering to make things right, or changing our behavior in the future.

For example, if you have frequently criticized your child's efforts, you may apologize and resolve to be more encouraging and supportive. If you've been disregarding your child's need for attention, you may make a serious effort to spend more quality time with them.

These behaviors demonstrate that repentance requires more than just words. It indicates to our children that we really apologize for our mistakes and are determined to change our behavior.

Modeling humility and regret means being open to feedback from our children. Encourage youngsters to express their opinions and feelings honestly, even if this means criticizing our acts or questioning our decisions.

This responsiveness to feedback involves a willingness to listen without becoming defensive, to consider our child's point of view, and to adjust our approach as needed. It also teaches our children the importance of courteous communication and seeking feedback from others.

Furthermore, modeling humility and repentance requires acknowledging our own need for God's favor. We are all flawed creatures who make mistakes and fall short of God's standards. We need His forgiveness, guidance, and ability to walk in righteousness.

When we publicly acknowledge our need for God, we teach our children the importance of humility and trusting in God's grace. We teach children that even adults need God's help and that it is okay to seek His forgiveness and guidance.

This openness can also improve spiritual interactions with our children. We can discuss our challenges and triumphs, as well as our experiences with God's love and forgiveness. We can encourage them to seek God's guidance in their own lives, confess their sins, and trust in His help to overcome problems.

Key Points

- → Grace is essential to create a safe and compassionate environment for punishment. It allows young people to learn from their mistakes without feeling judged or rejected.

- → Forgiveness is a powerful tool for healing and regeneration. It frees young people from the responsibilities of their past mistakes, allowing them to start anew.

- → Modeling humility and repentance is essential for building trust and connection. Admitting your flaws teaches children that they are not perfect and that it is appropriate to seek forgiveness.

- → Seeking forgiveness from your children shows responsibility and respect. It teaches children the importance of making amends and seeking reconciliation.

- → Guiding with grace demonstrates God's character and leads children to His unconditional love. It communicates that they are loved and accepted, regardless of their shortcomings.

<u>**Self-Reflection Questions**</u>

1. How freely do you forgive your child's mistakes? Do you carry resentment or animosity for them, or do you forgive their debt?

____

____

____

____

____

2. How do you handle mistakes in parenting? Do you own your mistakes and beg your child for forgiveness?

____

____

____

____

____

3. How do you model repentance for your child? Do you take steps to make amends for your mistakes and improve your behavior in the future?

____

____

____

____

____

4. How can you encourage your child to forgive themselves once they make mistakes? Do you remind them of God's unconditional love and forgiveness?

5. How can you create a more grace-filled environment in your home, where mistakes are recognized as opportunities for growth and forgiveness is readily given?

Chapter 6: Discipline as Discipleship

"Train up a child in the way he should go; even when he is old he will not depart from it." Proverbs 22:6
(ESV)

This popular proverb expresses the essence of discipline: discipleship. It highlights the importance of cautious instruction and the long-term power of instilling Christian values in our children's hearts. In this view, discipline is more than just correcting behavior; it is also about nurturing faith, shaping character, and forging a lifelong relationship with God.

Discipline as discipleship views every contact, instructional moment, and corrective action as an opportunity to draw our children closer to God. It is about incorporating faith into their daily lives, making it an integral part of who they are and how they perceive the world.

This approach recognizes that children are more than just miniature people who need to be taught rules and obedience. They are spiritual beings created in the image of God, with an intense longing for connection, meaning, and purpose.

Discipline as discipleship seeks to satisfy this spiritual hunger by giving children the tools and assistance they need to create a personal connection with God and prepare them to live a life that honors Him.

One of the most effective ways for disciples to build discipline is to incorporate spiritual exercises into their daily routines. These disciplines, including prayer, Bible reading, and worship, are more than just religious rituals; they provide opportunities to interact with God, experience His presence, and broaden our understanding of His character.

When we incorporate these disciplines into our family life, we create an environment in which faith is not just spoken about but lived out. We teach our children that connection with God is more than simply Sunday mornings and goodnight prayers; it is an integral part of everyday life.

Prayer is a powerful way to connect with and invite God into our lives. It enables us to express our gratitude, seek His guidance, and surrender our burdens to Him. When we pray with our children, we teach them to communicate with God, believe in His provision, and trust in His strength.

Setting aside time each day for family prayer enables us to incorporate prayer into our daily lives. This could involve gathering before meals, before bedtime, or at any other time that works best for your family.

Encourage your children to participate in these prayer sessions by sharing their prayers, expressing gratitude, and seeking God's help with their problems. You might also exhibit various forms of prayer, such as praise, confession, and intercession.

Bible reading is another vital spiritual practice that nourishes our spirits and broadens our understanding of God's Word. Reading the Bible with our children teaches them about God's stories, commands, and promises. We help children develop a love for Scripture and a desire to implement its lessons in their daily lives.

Family devotions are an excellent way to incorporate Bible reading into your daily schedule. Select age-appropriate Bible tales or chapters, read them aloud, and discuss their meaning and application. You can also use devotional books or resources to guide your discussions and provide further knowledge.

Worship is another powerful way to speak with God and express our love and adoration for him. Singing hymns, listening to praise music, or attending worship services together can create awe and surprise in our children, allowing them to witness God's beauty and majesty.

In addition to incorporating spiritual disciplines into your daily routine, discipline as discipleship means actively teaching your children about God's Word and instilling a passion for Scripture. This takes more than simply reading Bible stories and memorizing verses. It comprises assisting people in comprehending the meaning and application of God's Word in their everyday lives.

One way to accomplish this is through age-appropriate Bible conversations. Ask your children questions about what they've read or heard, encourage them to share their thoughts and feelings, and help them apply Scripture's teachings in their daily lives.

You can also utilize real-life examples to demonstrate biblical concepts. For example, *if your child is struggling with forgiveness, discuss the parable of the unforgiving servant (Matthew 18:21-35)* and the importance of forgiving others.

Another technique for cultivating a love of Scripture is to create a home environment in which the Bible is valued and respected. Keep Bibles easily available in your home, publicly display Bible scriptures, and encourage your children to read and study the Bible on their own.

You can also show your enthusiasm for Scripture by reading your Bible regularly, sharing your insights and discoveries, and demonstrating how God's Word applies to your life.

Discipline, or discipleship, is more than just imparting knowledge or enforcing rules; it is about developing a heart that loves God and desires to follow His ways. It is about creating a relationship with God that will guide your child through life's challenges and lead to a future full of meaning and importance.

Integrating Spiritual Disciplines

In the frantic pace of family life, where calendars overflow and demands compete for our attention, it's easy to neglect spiritual practices. We may find ourselves rushing through prayers, cramming in a few Bible readings, or skipping family devotions altogether.

However, if we want to raise children who are truly God-fearing, with a deep and meaningful relationship with their Creator, we must be intentional about weaving spiritual practices into the fabric of our daily lives.

These disciplines are more than just religious rituals or checkmarks on a to-do list; they are pathways to encounter God, experience His presence, and cultivate a healthy and growing relationship with Him.

When we prioritize these disciplines, we foster an environment in which religion is lived out rather than just discussed, God's Word is appreciated rather than simply read, and prayer is more than a formality but a lifeline to our Father's heart.

Prayer is an effective tool for connecting with God and inviting Him into our daily lives. It enables us to express our gratitude, recognize our mistakes, seek His guidance, and surrender our burdens to Him. When we incorporate prayer into our daily routine, we teach our children how to communicate with God, trust in His provision, and rely on His strength.

Setting aside time for family prayer is a practical way to incorporate prayer into your daily practice. This could involve gathering before meals, before bedtime, or at any other time that works best for your family. The goal is to develop a consistent rhythm that becomes an entrenched part of your habit.

Encourage your children to participate in these prayer sessions by sharing their prayers, expressing gratitude, and seeking God's help with their problems. You might also exhibit various forms of prayer, such as praise, confession, and intercession.

Another strategy for incorporating prayer is to pray spontaneously throughout the day. When challenges emerge, blessings arrive, or decisions must be made, take a moment to pause and invite God into the picture. This illustrates to your children that prayer is a constant connection with our Heavenly Father, not just at set times or places.

You can also assist your children develop their own personal prayer habits by providing age-appropriate resources like prayer notebooks and devotional literature. Encourage them to set aside time every day for peaceful reflection and conversation with God.

Bible reading is another vital spiritual practice that nourishes our spirits and broadens our understanding of God's Word. Reading the Bible with our children teaches them about God's stories, commands, and promises. We help children develop a love for Scripture and a desire to implement its lessons in their daily lives.

Family devotions are an excellent way to incorporate Bible reading into your daily schedule. Select age-appropriate Bible tales or chapters, read them aloud, and discuss their meaning and application. You can also use devotional books or resources to guide your discussions and provide further knowledge.

To make family devotions more engaging, incorporate artistic components such as storytelling, sketching, or acting out Bible stories. You can also use music, movies, or online resources to augment your devotional time.

Another method for incorporating Bible reading is to urge your children to read the Bible on their own. Give them age-appropriate Bibles and devotional materials, and create a quiet space where they can spend time with God and His Word.

You can also encourage Bible memorization by assisting your child in memorizing specific verses or sections that are meaningful in their lives. This not only helps children internalize God's Word, but it also provides strength and encouragement in difficult circumstances.

In addition to prayer and Bible reading, other spiritual practices can help your family's faith and your relationship with God. Worship, for example, is an effective way to express our love and devotion to God. Singing hymns, listening to praise music, or attending worship services together can create awe and surprise in our children, allowing them to witness God's beauty and majesty.

Serving others is another important spiritual discipline that teaches our children the value of compassion, generosity, and putting others' needs ahead of our own. Find ways for your family to serve together in your community, such as volunteering at a soup kitchen, visiting the elderly, or embarking on a mission trip.

Fasting is another discipline that families can practice together, though younger children may require additional explanation and guidance. Fasting means abstaining from food or other pleasures for a specified period to concentrate on God, seek His guidance, or profess reliance on Him.

Fasting, when done with wisdom and discernment, maybe a transformative spiritual experience that increases our bond with God and our reliance on Him.

Integrating spiritual exercises into your daily routine does not need adding extra tasks to your already overcrowded schedule. It's about making room for God in your family life, prioritizing your relationship with Him, and teaching your children to do the same.

It's about incorporating faith into your family's identity rather than only on Sundays or special occasions.

When you prioritize spiritual disciplines, you create an environment in which your children can experience God's presence, get a deeper understanding of His Word, and build a personal connection with Him that will last their entire lives.

You also give them an inspiring example of what it means to live a God-fearing life, complete with prayer, Bible study, worship, service, and a strong reliance on God's grace.

Nurturing a Love for God's Word

Every Christian parent desires to see their children develop an appreciation for God's Word, a passion for its truths, and a hunger for its insight. Nurturing a love of Scripture entails more than simply imparting facts or imposing rote memorization; it entails establishing a dynamic and personal connection with the living God who communicates through its pages.

This approach requires intentionality, creativity, and a willingness to meet our children where they are, both developmentally and spiritually. It is about accepting that their understanding of God's Word will grow gradually, like a flower blossoming petal by petal, as they mature and gather experience.

Young children experience the world through a lens of curiosity and imagination. Their minds are fertile ground for planting seeds of faith through captivating stories, vibrant images, and engaging activities.

Choose age-appropriate Bible storybooks with eye-catching images and engaging text. Read these stories aloud with enthusiasm, providing different voices to the characters and encouraging your child to participate in the storytelling process.

Encourage hands-on learning by drawing Bible stories, acting out scenes with puppets or miniatures, or singing songs about biblical principles. These interactive experiences let children engage with the stories on a deeper level, making them more memorable and meaningful.

Children's understanding and critical thinking skills improve as they mature. They begin to grapple with increasingly complex thoughts and pose deeper questions about faith and the world around them.

Introduce youngsters to different types of Scripture, such as the Psalms, Proverbs, and Gospels. Help students understand the historical and cultural context of the Bible, as well as how its lessons apply to their lives today.

Encourage them to question, voice their doubts, and battle for the truths of Scripture. Create a safe space for open and honest discussion, where people may share their opinions and feelings without fear of being judged or condemned.

This willingness to examine and doubt is critical for establishing a genuine love of God's Word. It allows children to connect with the Bible on an intellectual and emotional level, face its challenges, and discover its significance to their own lives.

Memorizing Scripture is a powerful tool for keeping God's Word in our hearts, allowing its truths to mold our thinking, direct our actions, and comfort us in times of need. However, memorizing must be done in an entertaining and meaningful manner, rather than just through mindless repetition.

Choose scripture that is relevant to your child's life and experiences. Help them understand the verse's significance and importance before they begin memorizing it.

Use novel techniques to make memory more pleasurable and engaging, such as setting verses to music, creating visual aids, or using interactive games and activities.

Encourage your child to apply the recalled Scriptures in their daily lives, showing how God's Word may provide guidance, comfort, and strength in everyday situations.

Another technique for cultivating a love of Scripture is to create a home environment in which the Bible is valued and respected. Bibles should be readily available throughout your home, with prominent displays on bookshelves or coffee tables.

Consider creating a designated reading nook or "Bible time" space where your child can read and study the Bible in a relaxed and comfortable manner.

Display Bible verses in prominent places around your home, such as the refrigerator, bathroom mirrors, and bedroom walls. These visual reminders can help your child remember God's Word and encourage them to think about its truths throughout the day.

You can also show your enthusiasm for Scripture by reading your Bible on a regular basis, sharing your own insights and discoveries, and demonstrating how God's Word applies to your life. Allow your children to see you turn to the Bible for guidance, comfort, and inspiration.

Discuss how God's Word speaks to you, challenges you, and guides your decisions. This authenticity may be incredibly beneficial to children because it shows that the Bible is more than just an ancient text, but a living and active source of wisdom and guidance for their parents.

Additionally, provide your children opportunities to engage with God's Word in the community. Attend church services with your children, join Bible studies or small groups, and encourage them to share their faith with others.

These communal experiences can help youngsters grasp how God's Word pertains to a larger community of believers, as well as how to use it to encourage, assist, and challenge others.

Nurturing a love of God's Word is an ongoing process that requires patience, creativity, and the ability to adapt your approach as your child grows and matures. It is about creating a faith-based culture in your family in which the Bible is respected, studied, and applied in everyday life.

Key Points

→ Discipline is more than just correcting behavior; it is about leading children to a lifelong relationship with God. Every interaction provides an opportunity for spiritual development.

→ Integrating spiritual exercises into everyday life helps children learn that faith is an important part of their identity. Prayer, Bible reading, and worship are part of their daily existence.

→ Teaching children about God's Word goes beyond memorization. It is about assisting individuals in recognizing its importance and use in their daily lives.

→ Creating a home environment that honors and respects the Bible encourages Scripture involvement. Accessibility and visual reminders can aid children in remembering God's Word.

→ Modeling a love of Scripture by example is an excellent way to influence children. When they see how the Bible has influenced their life, they are more likely to adopt it for themselves.

Self-Reflection Questions

1. How do you perceive the role of discipline in your child's spiritual development? Is it primarily about behavior modification, or is it a tool for discipleship?

____

____

____

____

2. How well do you include spiritual practices in your family's daily activities? Is prayer, Bible reading, and worship an everyday event in your household?

____

____

____

____

3. How do you teach your children about God's Word in an age-appropriate and engaging way? Do you go beyond memorization to help them understand the meaning and application?

____

____

____

____

4. What type of Bible-focused environment have you created in your home? Is the book valuable, reputable, and readily available?

____

____

____

---

5. How can you live your life with a passion for Scripture? Do your children see you reading, studying, and applying God's word in your daily life?

Chapter 7: Addressing Specific Challenges

"Be completely humble and gentle; be patient, bearing with one another in love." Ephesians 4:2 (NIV)

This verse from Ephesians illustrates the core of dealing with specific parenting challenges. It teaches us to approach difficult situations with humility, gentleness, and patience, knowing that our children, like us, are on a journey of development and learning. It reminds us that love should be the guiding principle in all of our interactions, even when dealing with difficult behaviors or stressful situations.

Parenting is a tapestry woven with threads of joy, laughter, and tender moments, but it also includes challenges that test our patience, wisdom and resolve. These issues may manifest as specific behaviors that undermine family unity, generate conflict, or inhibit a child's development.

Addressing these unique challenges requires a multifaceted approach that incorporates knowledge, judgment, and devotion to biblical principles. It is critical to remember that each child and scenario is unique, and there is no one-size-fits-all solution.

Sibling rivalry is a common problem for many parents. Sibling rivalry, jealousy, and conflict are all frequent experiences in family life. However, when these disagreements become regular or severe, they can undermine family unity and create a stressful situation for everyone.

Addressing sibling rivalry requires a proactive approach that emphasizes developing sibling relationships, fostering teamwork, and teaching conflict resolution skills. It is vital to cultivate a family culture in which each child is appreciated and respected for their unique features, comparison and competition are discouraged, and cooperation and mutual support are promoted.

When arguments arise, it is vital to respond kindly and fairly, aiding children in understanding their own emotions, listening to one another's perspectives, and developing solutions that benefit everyone. Teaching problem-solving skills such as compromise and negotiation can help children handle conflicts quietly and respectfully.

Contempt and defiance are also common issues. As youngsters gain independence and push boundaries, they may exhibit rude or defiant conduct. This behavior can be especially tough for parents since it undermines our authority and may trigger feelings of irritation or rage.

However, keep in mind that children regularly use disrespect and disobedience to communicate their needs, express anger, or seek attention. Rather than reacting angrily or penalizing, it is vital to address the underlying emotions and motivations that drive the behavior.

This could include actively listening, acknowledging their feelings, and recommending alternative ways to express oneself. It may also be vital to set clear boundaries, consistently implement punishments, and educate children on the importance of respecting authority and following rules.

Lying is another challenging behavior for parents to address. Children may lie for a variety of reasons, such as to avoid punishment, to gain attention, or to protect themselves from embarrassment or shame.

When a child lies, it is vital to confront the situation calmly and directly. Help youngsters learn the importance of honesty and the negative consequences of lying. It's also critical to address the root causes of the lie, offering support and guidance to help the child overcome any concerns or insecurities that may be contributing to their dishonesty.

In addition to these common behavioral disorders, parents may face unusual or complex situations that demand specialist attention and resources. These settings can include blended families, single parenting, and children with special needs.

Blended families frequently face unique challenges as they navigate new family dynamics, adapt to different parenting styles, and work to develop connections between stepparents and stepchildren. Open communication, tolerance, and a willingness to seek expert assistance can be quite beneficial in navigating these issues.

Single parents frequently face additional challenges as they navigate the duties of parenting alone. Building a strong support network, investigating community programs, and prioritizing self-care can all help single parents thrive while still providing a loving and stable home for their children.

Children with special needs may require additional assistance and understanding since they experience unique challenges and developmental variances. Seeking professional counsel, connecting with other families in similar situations, and advocating for their child's needs can all help parents provide the best possible care and support.

Individual parenting challenges require a combination of intelligence, insight, and trust in God's love. It is critical to remember that each child and scenario is unique, and there is no one-size-fits-all solution.

It is about seeking God's guidance, trusting in His strength, and knowing that He will equip us to confront the challenges of parenting with love, patience, and wisdom.

As we address specific difficulties, it is critical to remember that discipline is more than just correcting conduct; it is about guiding our children to a life of faith and holiness. It is about nurturing their hearts, shaping their personalities, and guiding them toward a deep and intimate relationship with God.

This approach of discipline helps us to look at our children through the lens of grace, recognizing that they, like us, are on a path of growth and learning. It requires us to respond to their faults with understanding, compassion, and willingness to forgive.

When we guide with grace, we create an environment in which our children feel at ease admitting their mistakes, asking our guidance, and learning from their experiences. We show them that our love for them is not dependent on their actions and that our acceptance of them is not based on their perfection.

This unconditional love and acceptance provides a solid foundation for children's growth and maturity. They learn that even when they fall short, they are still valued, appreciated, and beloved. This understanding enables children to take risks, try new things, and face challenges with confidence, knowing that their parents will always be there to support them.

Addressing individual parenting issues can be difficult and even daunting. However, it also provides an opportunity for growth, both for our children and for ourselves. It's an opportunity to strengthen our bonds with our children, rely more on God, and see the transformative power of His grace in our own and our children's lives.

Common Behavioral Challenges

Raising children is a beautiful experience filled with joy, wonder, and deep love. It is, however, an activity that will provide difficulties, putting our patience, wisdom, and resolve to the test. These challenges include typical behavioral concerns that many parents face, such as sibling rivalry, dishonesty, and stubbornness. These behaviors, while often accepted as typical throughout early development, can disrupt family unity, cause conflict, and hamper a child's progress if not addressed properly.

Sibling rivalry, the age-old dance of competition and conflict between brothers and sisters, is a prevalent subject in many families. It is typically driven by a child's innate desire for attention, acknowledgment, and a sense of belonging within the parental unit. When these standards are violated, whether real or perceived, disagreements can arise, leading to bickering, teasing, tattling, or even physical violence.

Addressing sibling rivalry requires a proactive and diverse strategy. It all begins with fostering a home culture in which each child feels cherished and appreciated for their unique features, where comparison and competition are discouraged and cooperation and mutual support are encouraged.

Parents can cultivate this environment by paying close attention to each child, carefully listening to their concerns, and appreciating their abilities and accomplishments. Avoid comparing siblings or exhibiting preferences, as this can lead to resentment and increased competitiveness.

Instead, emphasize the importance of collaboration by encouraging siblings to work together on similar goals, share responsibilities, and recognize one another's accomplishments. Allow siblings to connect and bond with mutual interests, games, or hobbies, fostering a sense of community and support.

When a quarrel arises, act calmly and fairly. Avoid taking sides or assigning blame. Instead, assist children in understanding their own emotions, listening to one another's points of view, and devising solutions that benefit everyone. Teaching problem-solving skills such as compromise and negotiation can help children handle conflicts quietly and respectfully.

Lying is another common behavior problem that can put a parent's patience and intelligence to the test. Children may lie for a variety of reasons, such as to avoid punishment, to gain attention, or to protect themselves from embarrassment or shame.

Addressing lying requires a delicate balance of firmness and understanding. It is vital to communicate clearly that honesty is a non-negotiable value in your family, and that lying has consequences. At the same time, it is vital to provide a safe environment in which children can admit their mistakes without fear of repercussions or judgment.

When a child lies, reply kindly but directly. Avoid making accusations or furious outbursts since these may make the kid defensive and less likely to disclose the truth in the future. Instead, express your disappointment and explain why honesty is critical for building trust and maintaining successful relationships.

Help the young person understand the consequences of their dishonesty, both in terms of the immediate situation and the potential long-term implications on their relationships with others. Encourage them to take responsibility for their acts and apologize by telling the truth and confessing their dishonesty.

It's also important to address the root reasons for the deceit. If a child lies to avoid punishment, assess whether your disciplinary approach is too harsh or if the child is uncomfortable admitting their mistakes. If a child lies to gain attention, consider whether they are receiving enough positive attention for their good conduct and accomplishments.

By addressing the root causes of lying, you may help your child develop healthy coping skills while also laying the groundwork for a relationship built on trust and honesty.

Defiance, or the open refusal to obey rules or requests, can be particularly difficult for parents to address. It frequently occurs as children develop their independence, challenge boundaries, and explore their sense of autonomy.

While disobedience can be frustrating, remember that it is usually a normal part of a child's development. Children must learn to express themselves, make their own choices, and assert their individuality. However, it is equally critical that students learn to respect authority, follow rules, and work together.

When faced with defiance, it is vital to remain cool and consistent. Avoid power struggles or escalating the situation through fury or threats. Instead, be upfront about your expectations and the repercussions of noncompliance. Follow through on those consequences consistently, even if they are inconvenient or onerous.

At the same time, it is vital to validate your child's emotions and acknowledge their need for independence. Give them options whenever possible, allowing them to exercise some power within specific constraints. This allows youngsters to feel acknowledged and loved while still maintaining parental authority.

Instead of dictating what your child must wear, allow them to choose between two outfits. Instead of asking them to tidy their room right away, give them a time restriction to complete the task.

This strategy allows children to have a sense of autonomy while adhering to the boundaries and expectations you have set.

Managing common behavioral disorders requires patience, awareness, and obedience to biblical principles. It is critical to remember that these actions are frequently a normal part of child development, not a personal attack or a sign of parental failure.

Unique Family Situations

While the fundamentals of biblical discipline are stable, their implementation varies according to each family's unique circumstances. In this section, we'll look at some specific family situations that may present unique challenges and how parents might adapt their approach to discipline while remaining grounded in God's Word.

Blended families formed through remarriage or adoption often face unique challenges. These families come from a variety of backgrounds, experiences, and parenting methods, making it difficult to maintain consistent discipline and negotiate new family dynamics.

One of the most challenging challenges in blended families is establishing clear roles and expectations for both parents and children. Stepparents may struggle to comprehend their position in the disciplinary process, whilst children may be confused or resistant to authority from a non-biological parent.

Navigating these issues demands open and honest communication. Parents should work together to form a unified front by establishing uniform rules and consequences and communicating those expectations to all children.

Stepparents should approach punishment with caution and tolerance, recognizing that building trust and rapport takes time. Building positive relationships with stepchildren, demonstrating love and support, and gradually becoming more involved in discipline can all aid in the transition and build a more peaceful family environment.

Single parents face great challenges in raising children without the help of a partner. This can result in several concerns, including financial stress, emotional exhaustion, and the constant juggling of multiple activities.

Discipline in single-parent households requires more awareness and resourcefulness. Setting clear routines, having realistic expectations, and prioritizing self-care can all help single parents stay consistent and avoid burnout.

Seeking help from trustworthy friends, family members, or community organizations can also provide significant encouragement and assistance. Connecting with other single parents can develop a sense of community and understanding by providing a venue for discussing ideas, offering support, and learning from each other's experiences.

Raising children with extraordinary needs has unique challenges and opportunities. These children may have physical, cognitive, or emotional issues requiring specialized care, therapies, and educational initiatives.

Discipline in these circumstances requires a detailed understanding of the child's unique needs and limitations. Working with therapists, educators, and medical professionals can provide valuable insights and guidance when developing effective disciplinary techniques.

Flexibility and adaptability are also crucial. Traditional disciplinary measures may not be effective for children with special needs. Parents may need to adjust their approach, emphasizing positive reinforcement, clear communication, and solutions tailored to the child's specific needs.

Patience and grace are crucial qualities in parenting children with special needs. Celebrating small victories, focusing on progress rather than perfection, and seeking help from other parents can all provide encouragement and strength on this road.

Regardless of the specific family situation, a few principles might assist parents improve their approach to discipline:

- Prioritize open communication. Create a safe space for family members to express their opinions, thoughts, and concerns openly and respectfully.

- Set explicit expectations and limits. Consistency and predictability offer children a sense of security and stability, especially in households with complex dynamics.

- Seek aid from others. Contact trusted friends, family members, or community organizations for emotional support, advice, and practical assistance.

- Practice flexibility and adaptability. Recognize that typical discipline strategies may need to be modified to match the unique needs of your family.

- Prioritize self-care. Taking care of your own physical, emotional, and spiritual needs will help you become a patient, caring, and intelligent parent.

Remember that God's grace is sufficient to meet any suffering we face as parents. He promises knowledge to those who ask (James 1:5) and authority to those who trust in Him (Isaiah 40:31).

Key Points

→ Each family is unique, thus disciplinary methods may need to be adapted to the specific situation. Blended families, single-parent households, and families with special needs children may necessitate unique methods.

→ Open communication is crucial in any family facing issues. Creating a safe environment for open and honest communication can help with dispute resolution and mutual understanding.

→ Consistency in expectations and limits is essential in complex family interactions. Predictability encourages children to feel safe and understand the rules.

→ Seeking assistance from others can give significant relief and encouragement. Connecting with friends, family, or community resources can offer advice and practical assistance.

→ When faced with unusual conditions, flexibility and adaptation are essential. Traditional disciplinary procedures may need to be adjusted to accommodate the unique needs of each individual.

Self-Reflection Questions

1. What specific challenges do you have in your family that may demand a more tailored approach to discipline?

____

____

____

____

____

2. How effectively do you explain these problems to your children and other family members? Are you allowing for open and honest dialogue?

____

____

____

____

3. How consistent are you in respecting standards and restrictions, especially under tough circumstances?

____

____

4. What support systems do you have in place to assist you with these challenges? Are there any resources you might use more efficiently?

5. How versatile are you in tailoring your disciplinary strategy to your family's individual needs?

Chapter 8: Discipline in Different Seasons

"Children, obey your parents in the Lord, for this is right. 'Honor your father and mother'—which is the first commandment with a promise—'so that it may go well with you and that you may enjoy long life on the earth.'" Ephesians 6:1-3 (NIV)

This verse from Ephesians highlights the need for obedience and respect for parents, a topic that continues throughout the Bible. It emphasizes that honoring our parents is not merely a moral obligation, but also a source of blessing and fulfillment. However, as children grow and mature, their perceptions of obedience and respect shift, necessitating that parents modify their punishment strategy to meet the changing demands and capacities of each stage of life.

Discipline in different seasons recognizes that children are not static beings; they are constantly expanding, learning, and growing. What works for a youngster might not work for a teen. Our expectations, boundaries, and disciplinary tactics must evolve alongside our children's growth.

Early childhood, which includes the toddler and preschool years, is a period of tremendous growth and discovery. Children are beginning to walk, communicate, and interact with their surroundings. They're developing their sense of self, pushing their boundaries, and testing their limits.

Discipline during this season is primarily about counsel and redirection. Young children are not yet capable of completely understanding complex rules or abstract concepts. Curiosity, impulsivity, and a need to explore their environment typically drive their conduct.

Clear and consistent boundaries are required throughout this phase. Create simple, easy-to-understand policies and consistently enforce them. Use positive reinforcement to encourage desired actions and redirect your child when they exhibit undesirable conduct.

Patience and understanding are crucial throughout this season. Young children are still learning how to regulate their emotions, so they may struggle to express themselves clearly. Tantrums, meltdowns, and defiant behavior are common as children gain independence and test their limits.

Respond to these eruptions with patience and tolerance. Help your child understand and express their emotions, offering comfort and support while setting clear boundaries. Avoid harsh punishments and disparaging remarks, as these can hurt their developing self-esteem.

As students advance through elementary and middle school, their cognitive abilities develop and their social world broadens. They start to understand more complex concepts, develop a stronger sense of right and wrong, and form closer ties with their peers.

Discipline in this season is more concerned with teaching, clarifying, and fostering responsibility. Children may now understand why rules and consequences exist, and they can begin to accept responsibility for their own decisions and actions.

Continue to establish clear standards and routinely enforce them, but also explain why the rules exist and what the consequences of breaking them may be. Encourage your child to create goals and make decisions, which will instill a feeling of responsibility and self-discipline.

Peer interactions are increasingly important during this season, and children may face challenges such as peer pressure, bullying, or social exclusion. Help your child navigate these social dynamics by teaching them conflict resolution strategies, encouraging positive friendships, and providing a safe space for them to express their emotions and worries.

Teenage years bring a whole new set of issues and opportunities for growth. Adolescence is a time when young people experience significant physical, emotional, and social development as they prepare for adulthood.

Discipline during this season requires a precise balance of education, support, and greater independence. Teenagers are developing their personalities, and values, and demanding increased autonomy.

Maintain open communication with your teenager and establish a comfortable setting in which they can express their views, feelings, and concerns. Actively listen, offer guidance and support, and recognize their growing desire for independence.

Maintain clear expectations and boundaries, but allow for greater flexibility and conversation as your adolescent gains responsibility and maturity. Involve children in decision-making processes, offer them a voice in family conflicts, and teach them to accept responsibility for their actions.

Peer influence can be stronger during adolescence, and young people may face challenges such as dangerous behaviors, social media demands, or academic stress. Provide guidance and support as they face these challenges, aiding them in making sound decisions, establishing healthy boundaries, and developing a strong sense of self-esteem.

Remember that discipline is more than just correcting behavior; it is about guiding your child toward a life of faith and virtue. It is about nurturing their hearts, shaping their personalities, and guiding them toward a deep and intimate relationship with God.

As your child grows, adapt your disciplining methods to meet their changing needs and talents. Maintain open communication, consistent guidance, and unfailing love and support.

Age-Appropriate Discipline

Discipline, like a well-tailored suit, should reflect the unique characteristics of each child's age and stage of development. What works for a toddler might not be appropriate for a teenager, and vice versa. As parents, we must be conscious of these developmental differences and customize our approach to punishment to our children's specific needs and abilities as they grow and mature.

Children in their toddler years are like explorers venturing into an uncharted world. Their curiosity knows no bounds, their energy is limitless, and their understanding of laws and consequences is continuously evolving.

Discipline at this stage emphasizes guidance and redirection rather than punishment. Toddlers are motivated by their perceptions and impulses, and their actions typically reflect their current desires and ambitions.

When a child misbehaves, it is vital to show tolerance and compassion. Avoid harsh punishments and lengthy lectures, as they are unlikely to be effective at this age. Instead, divert their attention, set clear limits, and explain why certain behaviors are undesirable.

For example, if a toddler is throwing a toy, calmly take it away and redirect them to another activity. Say, "We do not throw toys." "Toys are for playing nicely." Then offer something alternative, such as building blocks or a puzzle.

Consistency is key throughout this period. Toddlers thrive on routine and predictability. Create simple and unambiguous regulations, and then regularly enforce them. This defines what is expected of them and gives them a sense of stability and regularity.

As children enter preschool, their cognitive abilities improve, and their social world increases. They start to understand more difficult concepts, develop a stronger sense of self, and form closer ties with their peers.

Discipline at this stage can entail more explanation and reasoning. Toddlers may not fully comprehend the reasons for rules, but preschoolers grasp why certain behaviors are required and how their actions affect others.

When discussing misbehavior, explain why it was bad and how it made others feel. Encourage your child to express their feelings and perspectives, and help them brainstorm other techniques to deal with similar situations in the future.

Natural and logical consequences may also be useful at this level. Allowing children to experience the natural consequences of their actions, such as getting chilly if they refuse to wear a coat, can be a very helpful learning experience. You can also impose logical consequences, such as removing a toy if it is abused, to help youngsters understand the connection between their actions and the outcomes.

Positive reinforcement remains essential at this level. Praise and encouragement can help young people make better decisions and reinforce positive behaviors. Celebrate their efforts, acknowledge their victories, and express your pride in their growth and development.

As children advance through elementary and middle school, their social and emotional development improves. They become more aware of social norms, peer pressure, and the complexities of relationships.

At this stage, discipline should focus on responsibility, accountability, and self-discipline. Children may now understand how their actions affect others and begin to accept responsibility for their choices.

Encourage your child to create goals and make decisions so that they feel in control and accountable. Help youngsters develop problem-solving skills by teaching them to see potential consequences and make appropriate decisions.

When your child misbehaves, involve them in the process of seeking solutions and making amends. This collaborative approach instills in children a sense of ownership and accountability, allowing them to learn from their mistakes and grow in self-control.

Peer interactions are more important during this time, and children may face challenges such as peer pressure, bullying, or social isolation. Help your child navigate these social dynamics by teaching them conflict resolution strategies, encouraging positive friendships, and providing a safe space for them to express their emotions and worries.

Teenagers have a unique set of challenges and opportunities as they prepare to become adulthood. They are developing their own personalities, and values, and wanting greater autonomy.

Discipline during this era requires a precise balance of education, support, and greater independence. Teenagers like clear boundaries and expectations, but they also require the flexibility to make their own choices and learn from their mistakes.

Maintain open communication with your teenager and establish a comfortable setting in which they can express their views, feelings, and concerns. Actively listen, offer guidance and support, and recognize their growing desire for independence.

Maintain clear expectations and boundaries, but allow for greater flexibility and conversation as your adolescent gains responsibility and maturity. Involve children in decision-making processes, offer them a voice in family conflicts, and teach them to accept responsibility for their actions.

When your teenager engages in misbehavior, assist them to understand the consequences of their choices and develop strategies for making better decisions in the future. Encourage them to take responsibility for their acts, seek forgiveness when necessary, and learn from their mistakes.

Remember that discipline is not about controlling or punishing your child; it is about helping them toward a life of faith and virtue. It is about nurturing their hearts, shaping their personalities, and guiding them toward a deep and intimate relationship with God.

As your child grows, adapt your disciplining methods to meet their changing needs and talents. Maintain open communication, consistent guidance, and unfailing love and support.

Remember that you are not alone in leading your child through the many seasons. God is with you, empowering and guiding you every step of the way. He has promised to be faithful to all who seek Him, and He will honor your efforts to raise your child in His ways.

Spiritual Formation Through the Years

Spiritual development is the ongoing process of deepening our relationship with God, molding our personalities to reflect His image, and living a life that glorifies Him. As parents, we have the incredible privilege of guiding our children on this journey, supporting their faith, and helping them discover the depths of God's love and grace.

This process of spiritual formation manifests differently at each stage of childhood, as children's perceptions of God, faith capacity, and spiritual needs evolve with their physical, emotional, and cognitive development.

Curiosity, ingenuity, and simple, trusting faith are common characteristics of early childhood spiritual growth. Young toddlers are usually captivated by their environment, especially the spiritual realm. They are eager to learn about God, hear Bible tales, and explore the wonders of creation.

Parents can nurture their children's natural curiosity by introducing faith into their daily lives. Pray every day with your children, thanking God for His blessings and seeking His guidance. Read Bible stories aloud, bringing them to life with engaging voices and beautiful images. Sing praise and worship songs together, allowing music to express the joy and wonder of faith.

Children's understanding of God and ability to believe develops as they mature. They start to understand more complex concepts, ask deeper questions, and develop a closer relationship with God.

Encourage your children to share their thoughts and feelings about God by creating a safe environment in which they can ask questions, explore their doubts, and struggle with their faith. Help kids understand the Bible's lessons by applying the stories and ideas to their daily lives.

Allow your children to experience God's presence in nature, through acts of service, and in the community of faith. Encourage them to participate in church activities, assist those in need, and develop meaningful connections with other Christians.

Teenagers frequently go through a period of inquiry, discovery, and identity development. Adolescents may experience uncertainty, battle with faith, and want to understand their place in the world.

This season can be tough for both teenagers and parents, but it also allows for great spiritual growth. Encourage your youngster to ask questions, look into different points of view, and develop their understanding of faith.

Create a safe space for open and honest conversations on faith, skepticism, and life's challenges. Share your own faith experience, including your challenges and achievements, and offer advice and support as others navigate their path.

Encourage your teenager to participate in youth organizations, Bible studies, and service projects, which will allow them to meet other young people who are also exploring their faith.

Throughout these seasons, remember that spiritual formation is more than just passing on knowledge or imposing religious practices. It is about developing a heart that loves God, trusts in His promises, and desires to live a life that honors Him.

Key Points

> → Children's awareness of discipline and ability for spiritual growth develops as they grow. Disciplinary approaches should be tailored to the various stages.

→ Early childhood education emphasizes guidance and redirection. Clear boundaries and consistent replies help young children acquire acceptable behavior.

→ Growing up focuses on teaching and responsibility. Children can begin to understand why rules exist and accept responsibility for their actions.

→ Teenage years require a balance of education and greater independence. Adolescents need to communicate openly and respect their liberty.

→ Spiritual formation is a constant process that evolves with each season. Nurturing a child's religion requires adapting to their increasing knowledge and expectations.

Self-Reflection Questions

1. How well do your current disciplinary strategies match your child's age and developmental stage? Are your expectations and strategies reasonable given their current level of comprehension?

____

____

____

____

2. How can you address the specific challenges and opportunities for spiritual growth that your kid is experiencing in this stage of life?

____

____

____

3. How effectively do you communicate with your child about faith, morals, and life choices while taking into account their age and maturity level?

____

____

____

____

____

4. How do you strike a balance between guiding and supporting your child while also allowing them to develop independence and make their own decisions as they mature?

____

____

____

____

____

5. How can you encourage your child's spiritual development and help them cultivate a deep and intimate relationship with God throughout their lives?

____

____

____

____

____

Chapter 9: Creating a Culture of Faith

"As for me and my household, we will serve the Lord." Joshua 24:15 (NIV)

Joshua's passionate declaration encapsulates the spirit of creating a faith-filled environment in our homes. It is a commitment to prioritize God, make Him the center of our family life, and live by His values and goals. It is about creating an environment in which faith is not just an afterthought or a Sunday morning activity, but an integral part of who we are and how we live.

Creating a faith-based culture is comparable to building a house. It requires a solid foundation, strong walls, and a roof that provides shelter and safety. It's about consciously establishing an environment in which faith may thrive, where children feel safe exploring their spirituality, and where God's presence can be felt at every turn.

Creating routines that encourage faith and connection is one of the cornerstones of a faith-filled family. Repeating patterns and rhythms influence our daily lives. They provide structure, regularity, and stability, laying the framework for spiritual growth and meaningful relationships.

Family dinners set a natural pace for conversation and discussion. Gathering around the table allows you to share more than just food, but also stories, experiences, and beliefs. It's time to connect, hear each other's hearts, and strengthen family bonds.

Make mealtimes a priority, even amid hectic schedules. Set aside distractions such as phones and television so that you can engage with one another. Use this opportunity to share about your day, discuss your problems and achievements, and encourage one another in your faith.

Family devotions provide a focused time to study God's Word and grow in faith together. This could entail reading Bible tales, discussing a devotional book, or simply exchanging prayer requests and praises.

Make family devotions a regular part of your routine, whether daily, twice a week, or even weekly. Choose a time that works for your family, such as before bedtime, after dinner, or on Sunday evenings.

Maintain a nice and engaging atmosphere, encouraging everyone to engage by sharing their thoughts, asking questions, and praying together.

Shared activities promote enjoyment, laughter, and connection, so strengthening family bonds and creating lasting memories. These exercises can also be used to reinforce values, teach life lessons, and promote spiritual development.

Plan frequent group activities, such as nature walks, museum trips, or volunteer work for a local charity. Take part in interests together, such as athletics, painting, or learning a new skill.

Use these shared experiences to spark conversations about faith, values, and life lessons. Point out God's creation in nature, discuss the importance of serving others, and encourage your children to use their talents and capabilities to glorify God.

In addition to establishing rhythms, promoting a culture of faith requires creating a home setting that reflects your values and encourages spiritual development. This means being intentional about what you bring into your home, the activities you prioritize, and the conversations you have.

Choose media wisely, picking books, movies, and music that match your values and promote positive themes. Limit your exposure to content that is aggressive, sexually suggestive, or promotes negative values.

Set up a dedicated prayer room in your home, or display inspirational artwork and Scripture passages. Encourage your children to pray regularly, both individually and as a family.

Make time for rest and Sabbath, recognizing the need to set aside time for spiritual renewal and revitalization. This could be attending religious services, spending time in nature, or simply taking some quiet time to reflect and pray.

Be intentional about the conversations you have at home. Discuss your faith openly and honestly, including your challenges and successes. Encourage your children to question, express doubts, and share their own spiritual experiences.

Model a faith-filled life by infusing your beliefs into your daily interactions. Show your children what it is to love God, serve others, and live with integrity.

Building a culture of religion does not involve creating a perfect home or family. It is about intentionally establishing an environment in which faith is valued, encouraged, and lived authentically.

It is about providing a secure space for your children to explore their faith, ask questions, and develop their relationship with God. It is about creating a foundation of faith that will help them navigate life's challenges and lead to a future full of meaning and importance.

Remember, you are not alone in your efforts to create a faith-filled home. God is with you, empowering and guiding you every step of the way. He has promised to be faithful to all who seek Him, and He will honor your efforts to raise your children in His ways.

Establishing Faith-Based Rhythms

In today's fast-paced world, where schedules are filled and distractions abound, it's easy for families to drift apart, key relationships to fade, and spirituality to be pushed to the margins. However, by actively establishing faith-based rhythms, we may create a countercurrent, a steady pulse that unites our families, nurtures our spirits, and keeps God at the center of our lives.

These rhythms are the repetitive patterns and rituals that shape our days and weeks. They provide structure, regularity, and stability, laying the framework for spiritual growth and meaningful relationships.

Family meals set a natural rhythm for connection and discussion. Gathering around the table allows you to share more than just food, but also stories, experiences, and beliefs. It's an opportunity to reconnect after a long day, hear each other's hearts, and strengthen family bonds.

Make mealtimes a priority, even if you have a packed schedule. Set aside distractions such as phones and television so that you can engage with one another. Use this opportunity to share about your day, discuss your problems and achievements, and encourage one another in your faith.

Consider establishing a little habit, such as saying grace before meals or lighting a candle, to foster a sense of reverence and gratitude. Encourage everyone to participate in the discussion by sharing their thoughts and experiences and practicing active listening.

Family devotions provide a focused time to study God's Word and grow in faith together. This could entail reading Bible tales, discussing a devotional book, or simply exchanging prayer requests and praises.

Make family devotions a regular part of your routine, whether daily, twice a week, or even weekly. Choose a time that works for your family, such as before bedtime, after dinner, or on Sunday evenings.

Maintain a nice and engaging atmosphere, encouraging everyone to engage by sharing their thoughts, asking questions, and praying together. Use age-appropriate resources and customize your approach to meet your children's needs and interests.

Shared activities promote enjoyment, laughter, and connection, so strengthening family bonds and creating lasting memories. These exercises can also be used to reinforce values, teach life lessons, and promote spiritual development.

Plan frequent group activities, such as nature walks, museum trips, or volunteer work for a local charity. Take part in interests together, such as athletics, painting, or learning a new skill.

Use these shared experiences to spark conversations about faith, values, and life lessons. Point out God's creation in nature, discuss the importance of serving others, and encourage your children to use their talents and capabilities to glorify God.

In addition to these precise rhythms, consider incorporating other faith-based rituals into your family's daily schedule. This could include attending church services together, participating in Bible studies or small groups, or volunteering in your community.

Make Sunday mornings a special time to meditate on God and connect with your church community. Attend services together, participate in Sunday school classes, and fellowship with other believers.

Join a small group or Bible study to grow in your faith alongside other families. This allows you to discuss your challenges and triumphs, encourage one another, and grow in your understanding of God's Word.

Find ways to serve your community together, such as volunteering at a soup kitchen, visiting the elderly, or participating in a community cleanup project. These acts of service not only benefit others, but also teach your children the importance of compassion, charity, and putting their faith into action.

Establishing faith-based rhythms does not include imposing a strict schedule or religious behaviors on your kids. It's about intentionally making room for God in your family's life, including faith in your daily routines, and providing chances for spiritual development and connection.

It is about teaching your children that faith is more than just an afterthought or a Sunday morning pastime; it is an integral part of who you are and how you live. It is about creating a home in which God's presence is felt, His Word is cherished, and His love is demonstrated.

Maintain your flexibility and agility when establishing these cycles. Life is full of unexpected twists and turns, and you will have to change your routines or your plans at times. Don't be afraid to adapt your approach, find new ways to connect with God and one another, and maintain the rhythm of faith in your family.

<u>Cultivating a God-Centered Home</u>

A God-centered home is more than just a place where religious traditions are observed or biblical knowledge is imparted. It is a home in which God's presence pervades the entire environment, His ideals influence every interaction, and His love pervades every corner.

Creating such an environment requires forethought, a willingness to examine our priorities, and a dedication to merging our home life and faith. It requires making decisions that reflect our beliefs, engaging in actions that encourage spiritual growth, and cultivating an atmosphere in which God is acknowledged and His presence felt.

One of the most effective ways to create a God-centered home is to be mindful of the influences we allow into our living areas. The media we consume, the decor we display, and the activities we prioritize all influence the overall tone of our home.

Choose media wisely, picking books, movies, and music that match your values and promote positive themes. Look for things that encourage, inspire, and advance spiritual development. Keep track of your screen usage and ensure that it does not detract from opportunities for face-to-face connection, outside play, and creative inquiry.

Consider the sentiments conveyed by the decor and artwork in your home. Select goods that reflect your values, inspire beauty, and create a sense of peace. Display Bible verses in prominent places to serve as visual reminders of God's truths and promises.

The activities we prioritize have a significant impact on the environment at home. Set aside time for spiritually beneficial activities like family devotions, prayer, and church attendance. Encourage individuals to get involved in service projects, volunteer in their communities, and aid those in need.

Create a family rest and Sabbath schedule that includes time for spiritual regeneration and restoration. This could involve going to religious services together, taking a quiet afternoon for reflection and prayer, or simply getting away from the hustle and bustle of life to spend quality time with loved ones.

A God-centered home cherishes open and honest communication. Create a safe environment in which family members can express their thoughts, feelings, and questions regarding faith without being judged or condemned.

Encourage spiritual conversations by telling your own faith story and describing how God is acting in your life. Be open to your children's questions and doubts, and provide age-appropriate solutions and guidance as they explore their own beliefs.

Model a prayerful lifestyle by praying regularly, both individually and as a family. Encourage your children to develop their own prayer lives by teaching them to express gratitude, seek guidance, and surrender their burdens to God.

Make Bible reading a consistent part of your family's routine. Read aloud to your children, discuss the chapters you've read, and encourage them to memorize verses that are meaningful to them.

Show your children that faith is more than just a collection of beliefs or practices; it is a way of life that encompasses all aspects of your being. Allow them to see you embodying your religion in your daily interactions by being kind, caring, and truthful in all of your relationships.

Create opportunities for your children to experience God's presence in nature, through acts of service, and within the community of believers. Spend time outside together appreciating God's creation and marveling at His artistry.

Encourage your children to participate in service projects, teaching them the importance of helping others and sharing God's love with those in need.

Attend worship services, Sunday school classes, and youth groups to stay connected to your local church. Encourage your children to connect with other Christians, forming a community of support and encouragement for their spiritual journey.

Cultivating a God-centered home is an ongoing process that requires intentionality, consistency, and the willingness to examine our priorities and make changes as needed. It is about creating an environment in which children can witness God's love in action and sense His presence in their daily lives, rather than simply learning about faith.

Remember that you are not alone in your quest to foster a God-centered environment. God is with you, empowering and guiding you every step of the way. He has vowed to be faithful to those who seek Him, and He will reward your efforts to construct a house where He is adored and His presence is felt.

Key Points

→ A culture of faith is purposefully fostered, not by happenstance. It means making purposeful decisions that align with your values and prioritize God.

→ Setting up patterns that value faith and connection lays the groundwork for spiritual growth. Family dinners, devotions, and group activities can all help strengthen faith and relationships.

→ The media you allow in your home has an impact on your mood. Choose stuff that reflects your values and expresses pleasant emotions.

→ Creating a devotional setting encourages spiritual connection. Dedicated prayer areas and religious symbols might help keep God in the forefront.

→ Modeling a life of faith is an excellent way to influence your children. Allow others to witness your dedication to God via your daily actions and relationships.

Self-Reflection Questions

1. How intentional are you about fostering a faith-based culture in your household? Do your decisions and priorities reflect your values and beliefs?

____

____

____

____

____

2. How do you use rhythms and rituals to assist your family in fostering faith and connection? Are there any places you could improve?

____

____

____

____

____

3. How picky are you about which media you allow into your home? Is it in line with your values and promotes positive messages?

____

____

____

____

____

4. What steps can you take to create a more prayerful environment at home?

____

____

____

____

____

5. How well do you model a faith-filled life for your children? Do your actions and attitudes reflect your commitment to God?

____

____

____

____

____

Chapter 10: Equipping for the Future

"Teach them to your children, talking about them when you sit at home and when you walk along the road, when you lie down and when you get up." Deuteronomy 11:19 (NIV)

This Deuteronomy verse emphasizes the ongoing nature of discipleship, which entails incorporating religion into everyday family activities. It is a call to incorporate God's commands and teachings into our daily conversations, routines, and very being. As our children grow, this teaching takes on new dimensions, preparing them to navigate the world with knowledge, integrity, and a firm faith foundation.

Equipping for the future does not imply shielding our children from the world's difficulties or dictating their every move. It is about preparing students to make wise decisions, hold fast to their values, and live a God-honoring life in the face of adversity and temptation.

This preparation begins with teaching independence and responsibility. As children become older, they naturally want more autonomy and the capacity to make their own decisions. Our role as parents shifts from supervising their every move to teaching them to make responsible decisions and accept the consequences of those actions.

Surrendering responsibility can be difficult for parents. It needs us to relinquish some control, to believe that our children have assimilated the principles and ideals we have instilled in them, and to allow them to learn from their own experiences, even if this means making mistakes along the way.

Start by assigning age-appropriate chores at home. Assign tasks, teach them how to manage their time and resources, and include them in decision-making. As children demonstrate responsibility in these areas, their independence and autonomy will gradually increase.

Encourage them to pursue their hobbies and passions by providing them with opportunities to discover and develop their talents. Encourage children to set goals, work hard to achieve them, and overcome challenges.

Help them understand that true freedom does not entail doing whatever they want, but rather making smart decisions that align with their values and lead to a fulfilling life.

Equipping for the future entails preparing our children to confront the world's challenges with confidence and resilience. This includes not only teaching children what is right and wrong, but also supporting them in developing the character and abilities needed to deal with difficult situations, resist temptation, and stay true to their convictions.

Teach them to distinguish between truth and lies, to recognize the subtle influences of the world, and to make decisions that honor God, even if they are unpopular or difficult. Help children develop critical thinking abilities by encouraging them to question, examine, and evaluate information rather than taking it at face value.

Teach children conflict resolution skills such as good communication, respectful listening, and seeking peaceful solutions. Help them understand the importance of forgiveness, both giving it to others and receiving it from God.

Prepare children for the reality of adversity and tragedy by reminding them that while challenges are inescapable in life, God is always present to bring strength, comfort, and direction. Teach your children to seek God's Word for guidance and encouragement, to seek His presence in prayer, and to believe in His promises even amid adversity.

As our children mature, we shift our focus to preparing them to join the world with a strong foundation in their faith. This includes aiding them in forming a personal relationship with God that will sustain them through life's transitions and tribulations.

Encourage them to seek God's guidance in their decisions, to rely on His strength in their weaknesses, and to trust in His plan for their lives. Create chances for children to help others, use their gifts and talents to worship God, and make a positive difference in the world around them.

Help them understand that their faith is more than just a set of beliefs or rituals; it is a live, dynamic relationship with God that will evolve and deepen over time. Encourage them to seek out mentors, connect with other believers, and continue to learn and grow in their faith.

Introducing our children to the world can be a bittersweet experience. It's a time of excitement and anticipation as we see them work toward their goals and seize opportunities. However, it is also a time to let go and believe that they are capable of facing the world on their own.

Remember that you planted seeds of faith, nurtured their hearts, and provided them with the tools they needed to overcome life's challenges. Trust that God will continue to guide and protect them as they embark on this new chapter.

Continue to pray for them, offer your support and encouragement, and acknowledge their accomplishments. Tell them that you are always there for them, no matter what occurs in their lives.

Equipping our children for the future is an ongoing process that requires attention, patience, and a willingness to adapt our approach as they grow and mature. It is about preparing students to make sound decisions, hold fast to their beliefs, and live a God-honoring lifestyle.

Fostering Independence and Responsibility

Raising responsible and autonomous children is a gradual process that requires preparation, patience, and a willingness to relinquish control as they mature. It's about striking a balance between offering kids guidance and support but also giving them the freedom to make their own choices, learn from their mistakes, and grow into successful people.

This process begins in the early years, when we lay the framework for responsibility by establishing routines, communicating clear expectations, and allowing our children to contribute to the family. Even young children can assist with age-appropriate tasks such as storing toys, cooking meals, and sorting laundry.

Children's ability to accept responsibility improves as they mature. They can handle more complex tasks, manage their time and resources, and make more autonomous judgments. This gradual shift in responsibility not only prepares children for the challenges of adulthood, but also instills in them a sense of ownership, competence, and self-reliance.

Giving children control over their actions and decisions is one of the most powerful methods to impart responsibility. This means exposing children to the natural consequences of their activities, both positive and bad.

For example, if a child forgets to bring their coursework to class, resist the urge to deliver it for them. Instead, let them face the consequences of their forgetfulness, such as a lower grade or a missed opportunity. This experience, while maybe upsetting at the time, can be a terrific motivator for developing organizational skills and taking responsibility for their belongings.

Similarly, when children make sound judgments, thank them and acknowledge their efforts. Praise their initiative, acknowledge their hard work, and express your confidence in their abilities. This favorable feedback not only boosts children's self-esteem but also encourages them to continue making acceptable decisions.

In addition to allowing natural consequences, parents can teach their children responsibility by assigning regular tasks and activities. Assigning age-appropriate duties, such as setting the table, bringing out the garbage, or caring for a pet, can help youngsters learn valuable life skills while also making them feel like they are contributing to the family.

When assigning duties, be clear about your expectations, provide appropriate guidance and assistance, and praise and celebrate their accomplishments. Avoid using tasks as a form of punishment, as this can foster unfavorable relationships and diminish their value.

Allowing children to participate in decision-making processes encourages responsibility and independence. Engage youngsters in family conversations about household issues, vacations, and even money concerns. Give them actual options, such as picking their clothes, planning their weekend activities, or managing a small money.

As children demonstrate responsibility in these areas, gradually increase their freedom and autonomy. Allowing children to walk to school on their own, staying home alone for short periods, and organizing their calendars for extracurricular activities are all examples.

This gradual release of responsibility not only prepares children for the challenges of adulthood but also instills faith and confidence in their abilities. It demonstrates that you trust them, value their judgment, and are confident in their ability to make great decisions.

Fostering independence also means encouraging children to follow their hobbies and interests. Allow them to explore their talents, enhance their skills, and discover their unique characteristics. This could include registering children for extracurricular activities, providing access to literature and tools, or just encouraging self-directed learning.

As children pursue their interests, they develop a sense of purpose, accomplishment, and self-esteem. They learn to set goals, work hard toward them, and conquer difficulties. They also learn about their strengths and weaknesses, gaining valuable self-awareness for the future.

Supporting your child's pursuit of their interests does not mean dictating their path or steering them toward a specific job or goal. It is about providing them with the resources, support, and opportunities they need to reach their greatest potential and discover their unique purpose.

It is crucial to remember that gaining independence and responsibility is a nonlinear process. Your child will make progress, and then appear to regress. There will be moments of pride and accomplishment, as well as frustration and disappointment.

Throughout this journey, remember to show your child unconditional love and support. Celebrate their achievements, provide support during setbacks, and coach them when they fail. Let them know you believe in them, are happy with their accomplishments, and are always willing to assist them, regardless of the challenges they confront.

Fostering independence and responsibility is more than just preparing your child for the future; it is also about preparing them to live a fulfilling and meaningful life that is founded on their faith and guided by God's principles. It is about enabling people to make sound decisions, to use their skills and abilities to help others and to make a positive difference in the world around them.

Launching Young Adults with a Strong Faith

Introducing young adults to the world is a bittersweet symphony of pride, anticipation, and a touch of melancholy. It's time to celebrate their accomplishments, acknowledge their newfound freedom, and put their trust in the path they've chosen. But it's also a time to let go, to recognize that our role as parents has shifted, and to place our trust in the foundation we've laid and in the God who directs their pathways.

As Christian parents, our ultimate goal is not merely to raise well-behaved children, but also to prepare young adults for lives of faith, purpose, and service to God. This entails more than just passing on knowledge or enforcing rules; it entails developing a deep and abiding connection with God that will carry them through life's ups and downs.

One of the most essential things we can do for our young adults is encourage them to seek God's guidance in all of their decisions. Encourage them to pray frequently and seek God's wisdom in all of their decisions. Encourage them to read and study the Bible, allowing God's Word to influence their thoughts and actions.

Remind them that God has a plan for their lives that is far beyond anything they could imagine. Encourage them to trust in His timing, seek His will, and follow His guidance, even if the way ahead appears hazy.

As our young adults travel into the world, they will likely face challenges and setbacks. It is vital to provide youngsters with the strength and endurance needed to overcome obstacles while being committed to their religion.

Remind them that failure is not irrevocable, that mistakes are learning opportunities, and that God's grace is always there to help them get back on track. Encourage children to see obstacles as opportunities to learn, develop stronger, and enhance their faith in God.

Interact with other Christians, seek mentors, and foster a feeling of community within a local church to help them develop a strong support system. Encourage them to find accountability partners who will challenge, encourage, and support them on their spiritual journey.

As our young adults manage the complexities of relationships, work, and personal decisions, we must remind them of the values and concepts that inspired their youth. Help them understand that their faith is more than just a set of rules or beliefs; it is a way of life that should drive their decisions and shape their personalities.

Encourage them to form connections and engage in activities that will strengthen their faith and help them walk with God. Help them identify God's call on their lives, whether through their career choices, service to others, or family life.

Remind them that they should not live their faith alone, but rather in community with other believers. Encourage them to be active members of their local church, to use their gifts and talents to help others, and to be a light in the world, reflecting God's love and grace to those around them.

Launching young adults with a strong faith necessitates realizing that our role as parents is evolving. We must learn to strike a balance between our desire to protect and guide and our obligation to respect their autonomy and allow them to make their judgments.

This transition can be tough, but it also provides an excellent opportunity to see the effects of our parenting and appreciate the people our children have grown into. Give them your support and encouragement, but also allow them to develop, learn, and discover their path in life.

Continue to pray for your young adults, asking God to guide, protect, and strengthen their faith. Let them know that you are always available to them, providing unconditional love and support no matter what life throws at them.

Key Points

→ Equipping for the future necessitates a shift from direction to guidance. As children mature, parents go from making all decisions to empowering young adults to make sound ones.

→ Fostering independence and responsibility is crucial. Giving children age-appropriate responsibilities and increasing their autonomy helps them face life's challenges.

→ Developing resilience and character are critical components of preparing for the world's challenges. Teach your children how to evaluate truth, resist temptation, and stand solid in their values.

→ Launching young adults with a strong faith entails developing their relationship with God. Encourage them to seek His guidance, trust in His strength, and believe in His purpose.

→ As children get older, their parents' duties change. Respect their growing freedom and autonomy while offering support and advice.

1. How effectively do you strike a balance between offering direction and allowing your child to make their own decisions and face natural consequences?

____

____

____

____

____

2. How can you assist your child acquire responsibility and independence in an age-appropriate manner?

____

____

____

____

____

3. What specific skills and values do you inculcate in your child to help them face life's challenges with confidence and integrity?

____

____

____

____

____

4. How do you teach your children to seek God's guidance in their decisions and to rely on His strength in their weaknesses?

5. How do you promote your child's spiritual growth and help them create a personal relationship with God that will last their entire life?

Conclusion

As we conclude our exploration of God-fearing child discipline, it's important to evaluate the long-term impact this strategy may have on our entire family. It is about acknowledging that discipline, when founded on love, grace, and biblical principles, is an effective instrument for molding character, strengthening faith, and leaving a legacy for future generations.

One of the most significant benefits of a God-centered approach to discipline is the formation of a strong moral compass in our kids. When we continue to guide our children with love and wisdom, we help them develop a strong sense of right and wrong, a clear understanding of their values, and a desire to live a life with integrity.

This moral compass will serve them well throughout their lives, guiding their actions, shaping their relationships, and affecting how they interact with the world. It will teach kids how to stand up for what is right, resist temptation, and make choices that honor and reflect God's character.

Another key advantage is the development of a strong spirit. Life is inherently full of challenges, setbacks, and disappointments. A God-centered discipline method helps our children develop the resilience needed to face these obstacles with courage, hope, and perseverance.

When we teach our children to recognize mistakes as opportunities for growth, to seek God's strength in their weaknesses, and to believe in His plan even when things get tough, we prepare them to confront life's problems with confidence and resolution. We help children develop inner strength that will take them through adversity and empower them to conquer challenges.

Discipline based on love and kindness gives our children a profound and lasting sense of stability. When children understand that they are unconditionally loved, even when they make mistakes, they develop a strong sense of trust and belonging.

This assurance allows them to fearlessly explore the world, take risks without fear of rejection, and embrace their uniqueness without feeling pressured to conform to external pressures. It also gives children a secure place to go when they face hardships or make mistakes, knowing that their parents are always there to offer love, support, and guidance.

Furthermore, a God-centered approach to discipline instills in our children a sense of gratitude and humility. When we teach our children to recognize their dependence on God, admit their need for His grace, and accept His blessings, we help them develop a spirit of humility and gratitude.

This modest attitude will keep people from becoming conceited and arrogant, allowing them to recognize their own limitations, seek information from others, and give God credit for their accomplishments. Gratitude will fill their hearts with joy and contentment, helping them to appreciate the good things in their lives while also seeking meaning and purpose in difficult circumstances.

A God-centered approach to discipline benefits the entire family, not just our children's personal lives. When we prioritize faith, love, and grace in our parenting, we create a home environment that is calm, joyous, and respectful.

Our families transform into safe havens of love and support, where each member feels valued, understood, and accepted for who they are. We build profound bonds that withstand life's ups and downs, leaving a legacy of love and faith for future generations.

As we conclude this workbook, I'd like to convey one final message of hope and encouragement to all parents who are working to raise their children in a God-fearing manner. The task before you is not easy. It will require patience, perseverance, and a consistent reliance on God's grace.

Some days, you may feel overwhelmed, disappointed, or even defeated. There will be times when you question your choices, doubt your abilities, and wonder if you're making a difference.

Remember that you are not alone in these situations. God is with you, empowering and guiding you every step of the way. He has promised to be faithful to all who seek Him, and He will honor your efforts to raise your children in His ways.

Lean on Him for strength, seek His advice in prayer, and believe that He is working in your children's hearts, even if you do not see the fruits of your efforts. Remember that God's grace is sufficient to meet whatever challenge you face, and His love is unconditional for both you and your children.

Parenting is a marathon, not a sprint. It's a journey filled with joys and challenges, triumphs and setbacks. But it is also a great pleasure, an opportunity to collaborate with God to mold your children's lives and leave a Christian legacy for future generations.

As you continue on this journey, remember that your ultimate goal is not to raise perfect children, but to lead them to the perfect Savior, the One who loves them unconditionally and grants them eternal life. May your home be a place where faith grows, love abounds, and your children come to know and adore God with their entire hearts, minds, and souls.

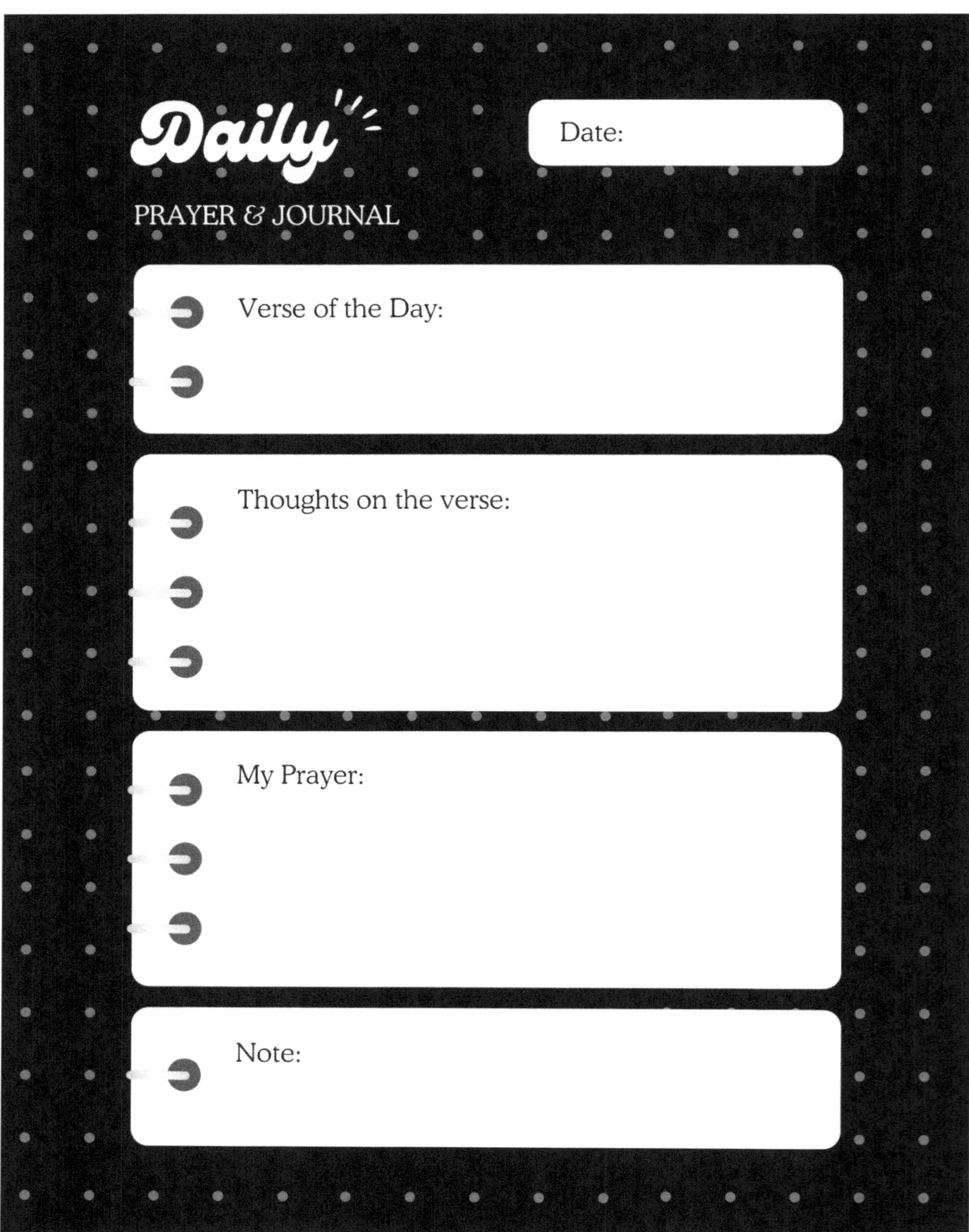

Daily
PRAYER & JOURNAL
Date:
Verse of the Day:
Thoughts on the verse:
My Prayer:
Note:

Daily

PRAYER & JOURNAL

Date:

- Verse of the Day:

- Thoughts on the verse:

- My Prayer:

- Note:

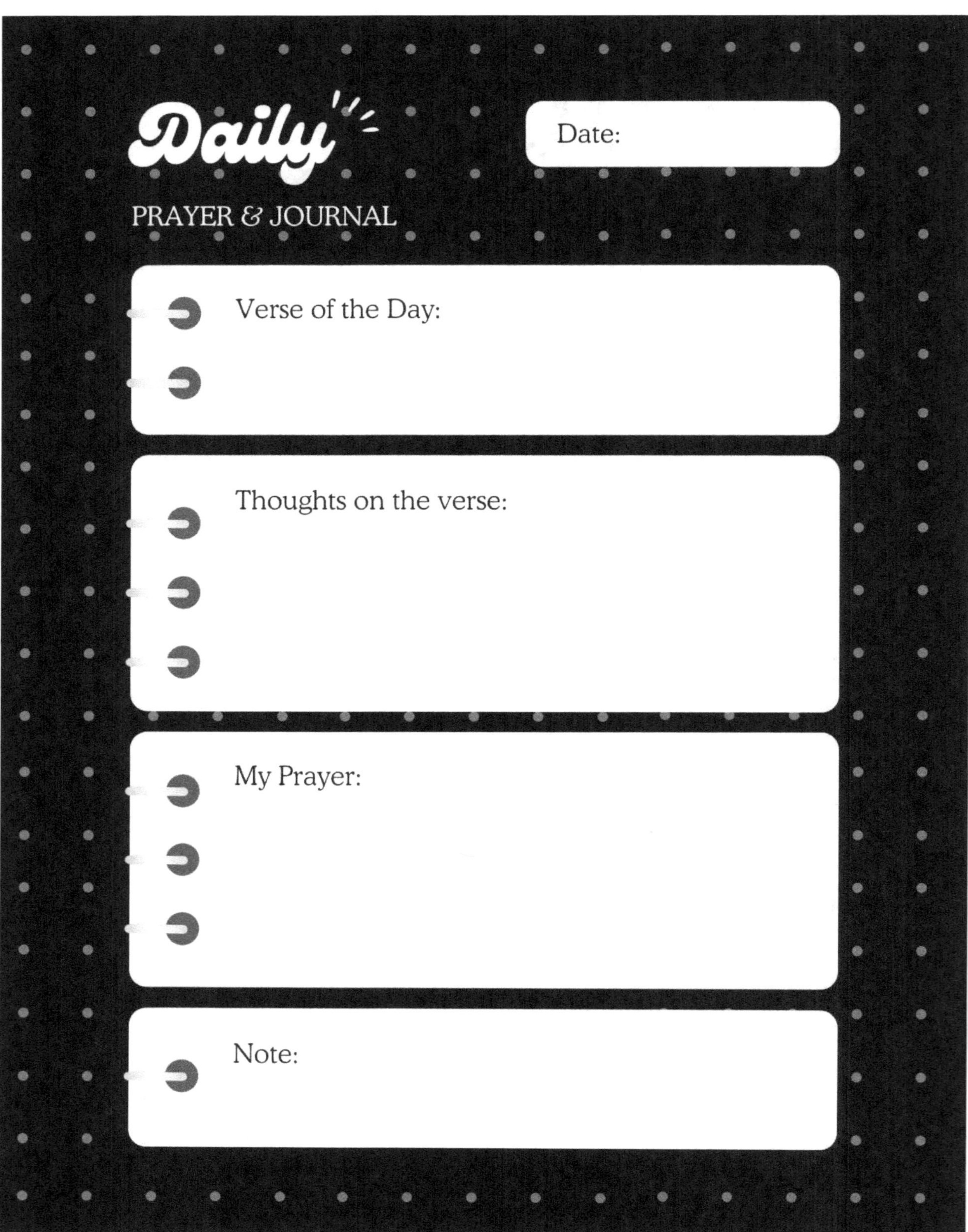
Daily
PRAYER & JOURNAL
Date:
Verse of the Day:
Thoughts on the verse:
My Prayer:
Note:

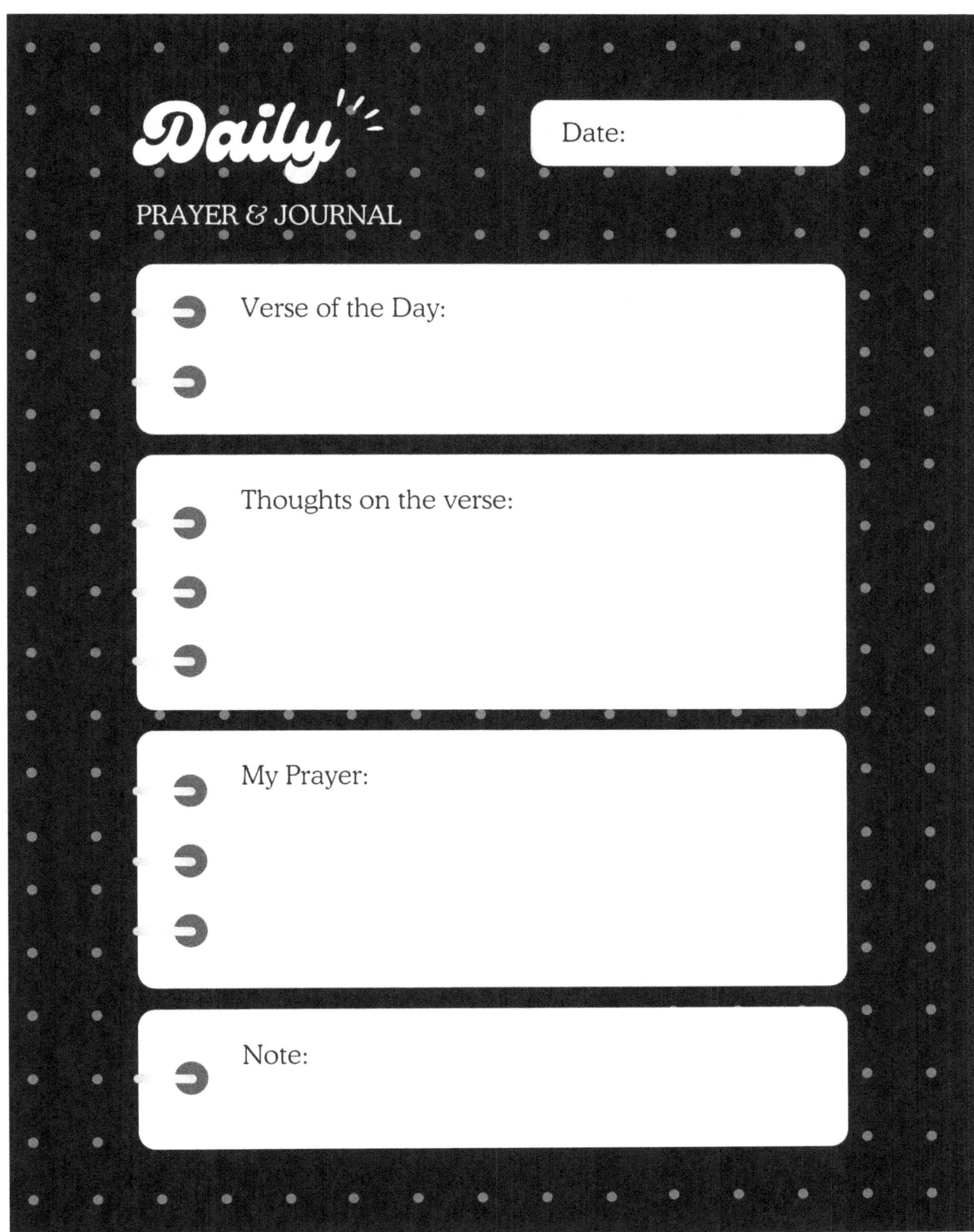
Daily
PRAYER & JOURNAL
Date:
Verse of the Day:
Thoughts on the verse:
My Prayer:
Note:

Daily

PRAYER & JOURNAL

Date:

Verse of the Day:

Thoughts on the verse:

My Prayer:

Note:

Daily

PRAYER & JOURNAL

Date:

Verse of the Day:

Thoughts on the verse:

My Prayer:

Note:

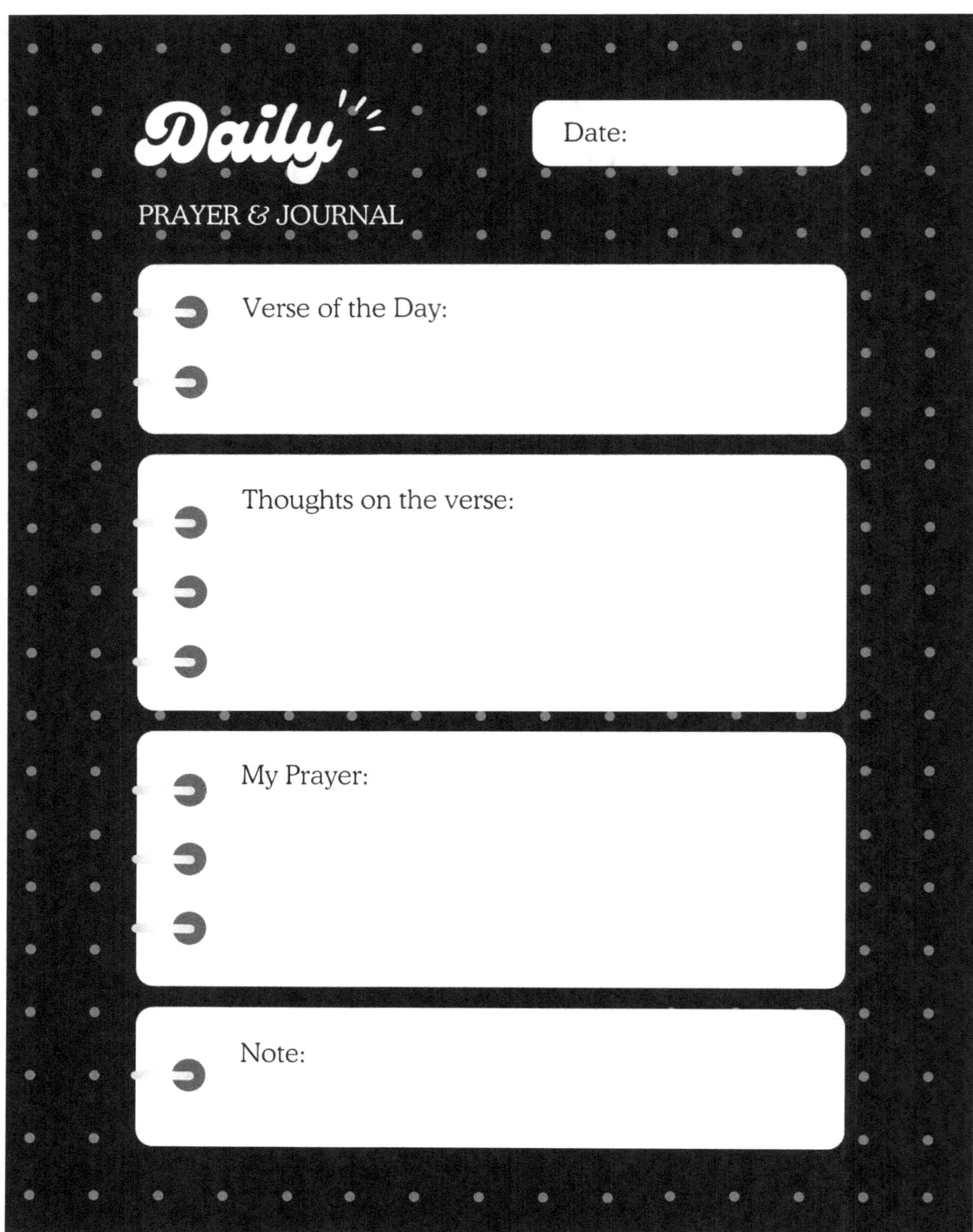

Daily
PRAYER & JOURNAL
Date:
Verse of the Day:
Thoughts on the verse:
My Prayer:
Note:

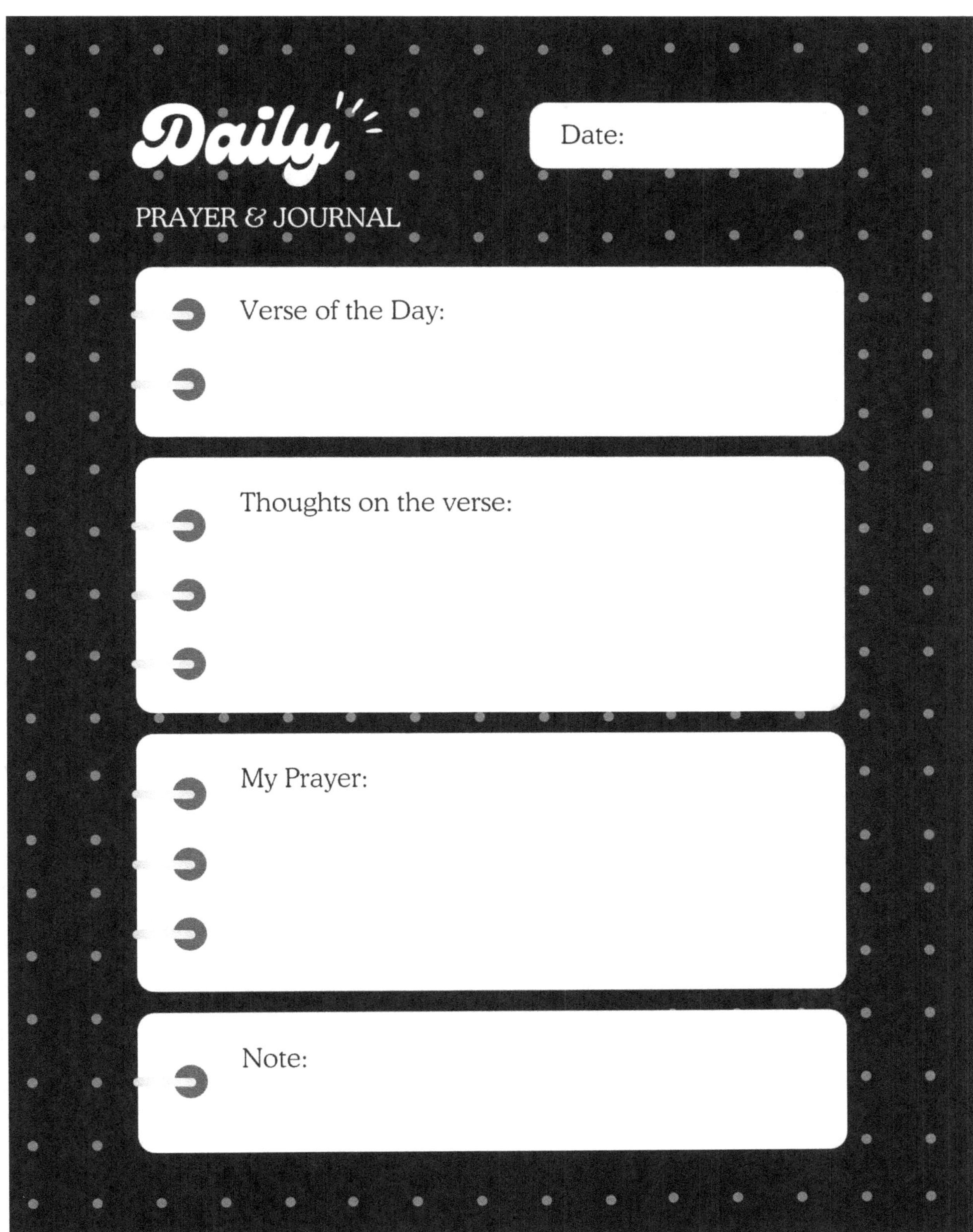
Daily
PRAYER & JOURNAL
Date:
Verse of the Day:
Thoughts on the verse:
My Prayer:
Note:

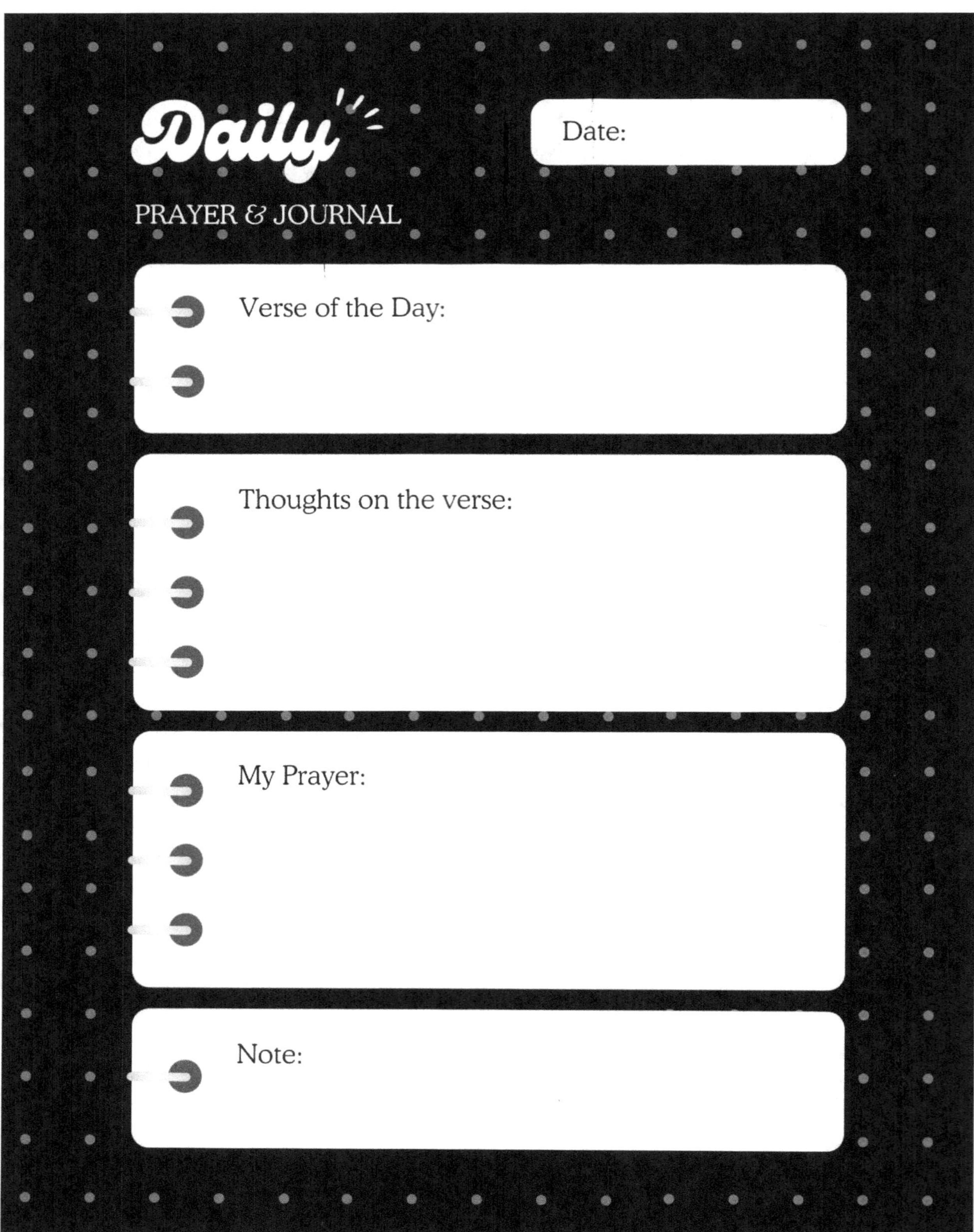

Daily
PRAYER & JOURNAL
Date:
Verse of the Day:
Thoughts on the verse:
My Prayer:
Note:

Daily

PRAYER & JOURNAL

Date:

Verse of the Day:

Thoughts on the verse:

My Prayer:

Note:

Daily

PRAYER & JOURNAL

Date:

Verse of the Day:

Thoughts on the verse:

My Prayer:

Note: